STORYTELLING

GARLAND REFERENCE LIBRARY
OF SOCIAL SCIENCE
(VOL. 302)

STORYTELLING
A Selected Annotated Bibliography

Ellin Greene
George Shannon

GARLAND PUBLISHING, INC. • NEW YORK & LONDON
1986

Library of Congress Cataloging-in-Publication Data

Greene, Ellin, 1927–
 Storytellling : a selected annotated bibliography.

 (Garland reference library of social science ;
vol. 302)
 Includes indexes.
 1. Storytelling—Bibliography. 2. Libraries,
Children's—Activity programs—Bibliography.
3. Children—Books and reading—Bibliography.
I. Shannon, George. II. Title. III. Series: Garland
reference library of social science ; v. 302.
Z718.3.G73 1986   016.02762'51   84-48877
ISBN 0-8240-8749-6 (alk. paper)

Cover design by Jonathan Billing

Printed on acid-free, 250-year-life paper
Manufactured in the United States of America

When the old man died, the shell was lost. In time, the shrine, too, disappeared. All that remained was the story.

But that is how it is with all of us: When we die, all that remains is the story.

Diane Wolkstein
White Wave: A Chinese Tale

CONTENTS

PREFACE

During the past fifteen years there has been a storytelling renaissance in the United States. The number of
articles about storytelling cited in *Library Literature*
in the 60s doubled in the 70s and seems likely to triple
in the 80s. We have drawn on this literature as well as
from the literature of education, psychology, folklore,
and anthropology to select significant books and articles
on storytelling published in English since the turn of
the century.

The purpose of this bibliography is to call attention to readings that deepen the storyteller's understanding of the function of storytelling in human development, give a historical sense of organized storytelling
to children in United States libraries, and offer practical advice on the selection, preparation, and presentation of stories. Our intent was to represent a variety
of styles and approaches to storytelling, from literal
faithfulness to the text to story seen as a continually
evolving art form, from the viewpoint that the story is
all important to spotlighting the performer or focusing
on the context in which the story is told.

Entries include (1) classic works that bear rereading and the best contemporary writings we could find on
a particular aspect of storytelling; (2) background readings to increase the storyteller's knowledge and respect
for this ancient art; and (3) a few ephemeral entries
that serve to show a significant trend but which may be
replaced by more substantive articles yet to be written.
Entries were chosen for their historical interest and
usefulness to contemporary storytellers. The emphasis

throughout is on story*telling*, but we have included a
short section on reading aloud. Reading aloud is a
good way for the beginning storyteller to gain confidence
and to introduce material that requires memorization,
such as poetry, literary fairy tales, and excerpts from
fiction.

Research was conducted with manual and computer
searches. Serendipity also played a part. From the
estimated 750 items we considered for inclusion we
chose 262.

Entries include monographs and sections of books,
journal and magazine articles, arranged under eight
categories: Beginnings, Purpose and Values, Art and
Technique, Storytelling in Special Settings or to Groups
with Special Needs, Reading Aloud, Storytellers, The
Building of Background, and Bibliographies and Indexes.
Some entries have been arbitrarily assigned but the Subject Index with its *see* and *see also* notes assure the
user access to all materials. Entries are organized
alphabetically by author within each category or by title
when that seemed more appropriate as in the case of a
special storytelling issue of a journal. Entries are
coded by consecutive numbers throughout the bibliography.
Journal citations include author and joint author, title,
journal, volume, issue, date, and pages. Sections of
books are cited by author of the selected material,
title of book, author or editor of the book, place of
publication, publisher, date, and pages. In instances
where an entry is known to have been printed in two
sources or reprinted, both sources are given. All
annotations are descriptive except for an occasional
statement of reservation or critical comment. Perhaps
a note about the section "The Building of Background"
(lifted from Ruth Sawyer's chapter headings) is in order.
This section includes material either too broad to fit
easily into the other sections or so narrow that it
seemed more appropriate to call attention to it by
assigning it to a separate category,

The Appendix includes a short list of films and
videotapes on the art of storytelling or storytellers
in performance and a sampling of storytelling recordings
on disc and tape. Non-print entries are arranged alphabetically by title. The bibliographic information

includes producer (and distributor, if different), date
of release if available, audiovisual format, color/black
and white if pertinent, and running time. Non-print
entries are not numbered or indexed. These lists are
short and easily managed. Their purpose is to call
attention to films and videotapes that can be used in
teaching and recordings (disc and tape) by well-known
storytellers, both living and deceased, that represent
different styles of telling and delivery. Users of this
bibliography are directed to other recordings by the
storytellers listed and to the catalogs of producers of
quality storytelling recordings, such as Caedmon, A
Gentle Wind, Spoken Arts, and Weston Woods. Non-print
materials on storytelling deserve a bibliography of
their own.

We would like to thank the staffs of the Joseph
Regenstein Library at the University of Chicago, the
Alexander Library at Rutgers University, the McIntyre
Library at the University of Wisconsin-Eau Claire,
Phillips Public Library, Eau Claire, and the New York
Public Library with special thanks to the staff of the
Central Children's Room and to Marilyn Berg Iarusso,
Storytelling Specialist. We also wish to express our
warmest thanks to our editor, Gary Kuris, for his
encouragement and patience. We invite users who do not
find their favorite books or articles on storytelling
within these pages to write to us, care of the publisher,
with suggestions of entries for future editions.

INTRODUCTION

Storytelling has been called the oldest and the newest
of the arts. Human beings seem to have an inbuilt need
to structure their world and to communicate their feelings and experiences through storying. Lewis Carroll
called stories "love gifts." It was an apt description,
for stories offer pleasure, release, and sustenance for
the spirit-self. Scholars believe that the first stories
were told in the first person. They may have been expressions of pride or exultation over some act of bravery
or accomplishment, such as this early chant from Green-
land:

> I, Keokok, have slain a bear.
> Ayi-ayi-ayi--
> A great bear, a fierce bear,
> Ayi-ayi-ayi--
> With might have I slain him.
> Ayi-ayi-ayi--
> Great are the muscles of my arm--
> Strong for spear throwing--
> Strong for bear slaying--
> Strong for kayak going--
> I, Keokok, have slain a bear.
> Ayi-ayi-ayi--[1]

They may have been chants to accompany repetitive tasks,
such as grinding corn or sharpening weapons for hunting.
Human beings wondered how the world came into being and
created myths. In this early period *everyone* was a
storyteller just as every young child today is a story-

teller. The three-year-old tells a story using gestures, mime, dance, sound, and language, as in an earlier age when the expressive arts were one. As human societies became more complex, art specialties--drama, dance, music--developed. Song separated from narration. Those persons who possessed charisma, a greater command of language, a good memory, and a fine sense of timing, became the community's storytellers. Stories changed from first-person to third-person narratives. One theory is that deeds were enlarged upon so much that modesty required the teller to attribute them to a third party and thus the hero tale was created. Storytellers became the historians and keepers of the culture as well as its entertainers. By the fifth century A.D. there were schools in Ireland and Wales to train storytellers, and master storytellers were elevated to positions of great power. The king's storyteller rode beside him in battle and, if captured, his ransom was the handsome sum of 400 head of cattle. In Ireland the ollams, or master storytellers, were allowed to wear five colors, only one less than royalty, while more common folk could wear only one, two, three, or four colors, depending on their social standing. The ollums were also entitled to wear a cloak made of many-colored bird feathers. In Europe storytellers reached the height of their power during the Middle Ages from the tenth to the fourteenth centuries. With the invention of the printing press in 1450 the oral tradition began to wane, especially among the upper classes and the new middle class who were able to afford books. The storyteller's role as historian and newsbearer was usurped by the print media. Irish storyteller and poet Padraic Colum believed the extension of the day's rhythm into night also contributed to the waning of storytelling. Before daylight was extended by artificial means day and night rhythms were very different and long dark nights lent themselves to storytelling. The ascendance of science in western society served to question literary wisdom. Storytelling gradually lost its spiritual force and became mere entertainment. Eventually folk stories were relegated to the nursery where they were preserved for the folklorists to rediscover in the nineteenth century. The Brothers Grimm revived an interest in the oral tradition when they

collected stories from oral sources and published their
collection *Kinder und Hausmärchen* (1812-1815). Their
methodology has been criticized by modern folklorists
but their work encouraged others and accelerated the
science of folklore. Even more important as Anne
Pellowski notes in her scholarly survey, *The World of
Storytelling*, "the Grimm tales must be considered as the
single most important group of folk stories that affected storytelling for children. Their widespread appeal
and their contemporaneous legitimacy helped European
parents to believe it was important to continue telling
stories to children, even though, in some cases, there
was opposition from educational authorities."[2] The great
German educator, Friedrich Froebel, may have been favor-
ably impressed by the Brothers Grimm, for storytelling
was an important part of the kindergarten program he
founded in 1837. The kindergarten movement spread with
the German immigrants and in 1873 the first kindergarten
was incorporated into a public school system in the
United States. Sara Cone Bryant, a kindergarten teacher,
wrote the first storytelling text published in the United
States. The book was *How to Tell Stories to Children*,
published by Houghton Mifflin & Co. in 1905.

    Changes in attitude toward children and several
social movements that occurred in the United States
during the latter half of the nineteenth century and the
early part of the twentieth century encouraged storytelling to children. These included the development of playgrounds, settlement houses, Sunday Schools, the founding
of the YMCA in 1851 and the YWCA in 1866, the Boy Scouts
in 1910 and the Girl Scouts in 1912, and the American
Library Association in 1876 with a special division for
librarians serving children formed in 1900. Two influ-
ential educators, John Dewey and G. Stanley Hall, were
strong supporters of storytelling to children. Instruc-
tion in storytelling was given in the kindergarten
training schools and at library schools, and in particular, at the Pratt Institute Library School and the
Carnegie Library School in Pittsburgh. In 1903 a group
of teachers attending summer school in Knoxville,
Tennessee, founded the National Story Tellers' League.
Richard T. Wyche founded and edited the League's journal,

The Storytellers'. Magazine, served as president of the
League, and wrote the second book of storytelling to be
published in the United States, *Some Great Stories and
How to Tell Them* (Newson & Co., 1910). It is interesting to note that the two most vigorous storytelling
organizations in the United States--the forementioned
National Story Tellers' League and the National Association for the Preservation and Perpetuation of Storytelling (NAPPS) formed in the 1970s--began in Tennessee.

The exact date of the first library story hour is
uncertain, but it was sometime during the last part of
the nineteenth century. Anne Carroll Moore, then
Children's Librarian at the Pratt Institute Free Library
in Brooklyn, held informal story hours as early as 1896.
By 1899 both the Carnegie Library of Pittsburgh (the
library with the strongest claim for the first system-
atized story hour program) and the Buffalo (N.Y.) Public
Library were holding story hours on a regular basis.
Elizabeth Botset of the Carnegie Library of Pittsburgh,
in an article published in *Carnegie Magazine* in 1933,
gives credit to another Carnegie librarian, Charlotte
Keith Bissell, for the origin of library story hours.
According to Botset, Bissell noticed a group of younger
children listlessly leafing through picture books in the
library. She wondered what the result would be if a
librarian *told* stories to such children and why the
story hour, so successful in hospitals, had not been
tried in libraries to introduce books.

Marie Shedlock's visit to New York at the turn of
the century gave library storytelling the impetus it
needed. Marie Shedlock was born in France and grew up
in England. She was a teacher of young children for
many years before becoming a professional storyteller
in 1890. Shedlock came to America to tell the stories
of Hans Christian Andersen (in French) to the children
of the well-to-do at Sherry's, a fashionable restaurant
in Manhattan. Mary Wright Plummer, director of the
School of Library Science at Pratt Institute in
Brooklyn, heard Marie Shedlock and invited her to tell
stories to the trustees, directors, and faculty of
Pratt. Anne Carroll Moore thought the children at Pratt
should have the pleasure of hearing Miss Shedlock, too,

so on a snowy Saturday morning in January 1903 Marie
Shedlock returned to Pratt. When the program was over,
a small girl asked Miss Moore, "Is she a fairy, or just
a lady?" Anne Carroll Moore later wrote, "There was
never any doubt in my mind after that morning that a
children's library should have a regular story hour."[3]

Marie Shedlock pursued storytelling as an art. She
did not use the affected speech which was in vogue at
the time nor was she didactic. She inspired others to
become storytellers, among them Anna Cogswell Tyler,
Miss Moore's assistant at Pratt, who became the first
supervisor of storytelling at the New York Public Library, Mary and John Cronan who carried out a storytelling program in Boston schools and libraries for over
half a century, and Ruth Sawyer, one of America's best
known storytellers. Shedlock travelled extensively in
the United States, lecturing on the art of storytelling
in New York, Boston, Pittsburgh, Chicago, and the West
Coast. She wrote a book, *The Art of the Story-Teller*
(D. Appleton & Co., 1915), which became a classic in its
field.

Another storyteller who influenced the manner in
which stories were told in libraries was Gudrun Thorne-
Thomsen. Whereas Shedlock's style was literary,
Thorne-Thomsen used a folkloric mode, but both women
emphasized simplicity, careful selection, and reliance
on the human voice alone to convey the nuances of the
story. Gudrun Thorne-Thomsen was born in Norway, the
daughter of an actress noted for her portrayal of the
women in Henrik Ibsen's plays. Gudrun Thorne-Thomsen
came to Chicago when she was fifteen and trained to be
a teacher at the Cook County Normal School. There she
met Colonel Francis W. Parker whom John Dewey called
"the father of progressive education." Later Parker
and Dewey and Thorne-Thomsen joined the faculty of the
University of Chicago Laboratory Schools. The Laboratory
Schools were Froebel-inspired and storytelling was promi-
nent in the curriculum. William Rainey Harper, active
in the Chautauqua movement and a storyteller himself,
was then president of the University of Chicago. Thorne-
Thomsen believed that imaging exercises and listening to
oral literature prepared children for reading. When
children became stuck in decoding, Thorne-Thomsen rec-

ommended that their teacher abandon any further effort at
that task and tell the children stories instead. This
insight into the relationship of oral literature,
imaging, and reading, shared by Thorne-Thomsen, Parker,
Dewey, and Harper, was lost for many years while schools
emphasized the technical aspects of reading.

The close connection between storytelling and reading is characteristic of library storytelling. From
the beginning, the "proper function of the library story
hour was to introduce children to the best kind of books
and to arouse a desire for a wider reading range." The
Carnegie Library at Pittsburgh, for instance, became
famous for its story hour cycles on Greek myths, Norse
mythology, and hero tales. Storytelling was thought
of as a form of reading guidance. Stories were selected
from books on the library shelves on the assumption that
story hour listeners would then want to read the stories
for themselves. Circulation figures seem to bear this
out. The children's librarian at the Cleveland Public
Library noted in her annual report for 1909 that Hans
Christian Andersen's *The Snow Queen* circulated 93 times
at the two branches where the story was told at story
hour compared to four circulations at the two branches
where it had not been told. Such early reports show
that the keeping of statistics to justify library
programs is not new.

Storytelling in libraries was widely accepted though
it was not without its critics. John Cotton Dana, then
librarian of the Newark, N.J., Public Library and past
president of the American Library Association, thought
storytelling was the responsibility of the schools and
considered it an ill use of the librarian's time and
energy. Writing for *Public Libraries* in 1908 Dana
labeled library-storytellers "altruistic, emotional,
dramatic, irrepressible childlovers who do not find
ordinary library work gives sufficient opportunities for
altruistic indulgence."[4] He advised any library that
could spare such misguided souls "to set them at teaching
the teachers the art of storytelling." Fortunately,
Dana's opinion reflected a minority point of view and
library storytelling flourished. Children's librarians
went out into the schools, playgrounds, and other recre-

ational centers to tell stories, as reported in Miss
Moore's "Report of the Committee on Storytelling,"
published in *Playground* in 1910.

Before leaving this early period it is worth noting,
as Richard Alvey pointed out in his doctoral dissertation[5] on organized storytelling to children in the United
States, that approximately 1,000,000 immigrants entered
the United States each year from 1900 to 1913. Librarians looked on storytelling as a way of integrating so
many diverse heritages and of teaching English and the
English language orally. Libraries in ports of entry,
particularly New York and Boston, carried out extensive
programs among immigrants. This is one of several paral-
lels the writer sees between library work with children
today and library work during the early part of our
century. In 1911 the Boston Public Library hired Mrs.
Mary W. Cronan, a kindergarten teacher trained in the
Froebel method and an experienced storyteller. She was
joined by her husband, John, and her siser, Mrs. Margaret
Powers. The trio told the tales of knighthood and epics
of heroes and saints to the children of immigrants.

Alvey also noted the conflict between storytelling
as an art and storytelling as an educational device or a
way to increase book circulation. There were few librarians like Edna Lyman Scott who publicly stated that
storytelling was "an art in itself, with the great under-
lying purpose of all art, to give joy to the world," and
that "only as storytelling" was given "its real place in
the world of art" could it attain "its full significance."[6] Nevertheless, librarians who had been influenced by the artistry of Marie Shedlock and Gudrun
Thorne-Thomsen believed that storytelling demanded creative effort and discipline. They did not use storytelling in a didactic way as did many teachers who had turned
away from Froebel's approach to storytelling. The
library-storyteller was considered an interpreter of
literature for children. Her goal was "to cultivate a
capacity for literary appreciation." This attitude,
which continues to the present day, was expressed by
Alice M. Jordan, head of children's work at the Boston
Public Library in her article published in the first
Storytelling Issue of *The Horn Book Magazine* (May 1934).

Miss Jordan wrote: "There is, as we know, a sensitive-
ness to the magic of words natural in some children,
while in others it waits to be wakened.... Out of the
repetition of melodious expressions as they reach the
ear comes an appreciation of language not easily gained
from the printed page."[7]

The first library story hours were planned for
children age nine and older. By that age children were
expected to have mastered the mechanics of reading, but
librarians noticed that at about the same age children
began to lose interest in reading. Picture book hours
for children age five to seven started at the Carnegie
Library of Pittsburgh as early as 1902 and other libraries soon followed suit. Library story hours for children
of school age reached a peak in the twenties. In 1920
Jordan estimated that the Cronans were telling stories
to 1800 library listeners per week as well as to four
thousand classroom pupils in auditorium groups. Attendance at Carnegie Library story hours peaked in 1924 at
nearly 150,000. But a shift was taking place from the
oral tradition to the printed word. The National Story
Tellers' League changed its emphasis from story*telling*
to *stories* and in so doing weakened its influence on the
direction of storytelling in America. In 1919 Macmillan
created the first juvenile department in a publishing
house. Other publishers soon followed. *The Horn Book
Magazine*, a literary journal, and *Elementary English
Review* (now *Language Arts*), began publication in 1924.
The influx of illustrators from Europe after World War
I--artists influenced by the Impressionists and Expres-
sionists, Cubists, and other Postimpressionists who
brought with them a rich tradition--and the development
of better methods of reproducing art in books set the
stage for the flowering of the American picture book.
This was the period, too, of the early childhood movement. Lucy Sprague Mitchell spearheaded the "here" and
"now" school of publishing--"here" and "now" meaning the
familiar and immediate. In 1935 the Detroit Public
Library began picture book hours for preschoolers age
three to five. From here on attendance at library story
hours for school age children declined and were scheduled
less frequently. The proliferation of organized activities competed for the children's attention and greater

demands made on children's librarians left less time for story hour preparation. Though perhaps still unaware of what was happening, the library profession--along with the general society--was moving toward an emphasis on information. In 1939 Elizabeth Nesbitt, then Associate Professor of Library Science at Carnegie Library School, made an eloquent plea for the continuation of the library story hour and the importance of the storyteller as an interpreter of literature for the child. Nesbitt carefully distinguished between reading for information and reading for literary appreciation. The 40s and 50s saw an increase in publication of informational books for children, accelerated in 1957 when the Russians launched Sputnik and interest in science skyrocketed. Library story hours for ages three to five flourished under the baby boom of the 50s, but time needed for preparation for story hour for older boys and girls was suspect in an increasingly scientifically oriented society and a cost-effective economy. "Realists" questioned the value of imaginative stories in the child's development and spoke out against violence in the folk tales.

The 60s brought both political and social upheaval. Consciousness-raised librarians reached out into the community with a fervor matched only by the pioneer library-storytellers at the turn of the century. They held stair-step story hours in urban ghettoes and worked with Head Start teachers. Some of the children who attended these programs came from cultures rich in the oral tradition. A greater number were born into families that had neither an oral nor a written tradition. Librarians sought simpler story books to use with pre-schoolers who were not used to being read to at home. Music, especially the singing of folk songs, was added to the story hour program. Programs became less literary and less structured. Multimedia story hours and pure film programs became increasingly popular in a society that was becoming more visually oriented and with a child population that had grown up with television.

Jean Piaget, the eminent Swiss psychologist who received recognition in Europe in the 1930s for his theories of cognitive development, was becoming known to Americans through translations and interpretations

of his writings. Betty Weeks, an early childhood educator at the National College of Education in Evanston,
Illinois, believes listening to stories helps children
in the two processes Piaget considered most important
for human functioning--assimilation and accomodation.
She relates this anecdote: a few weeks after telling her
kindergarten class the story of Persephone, on a brisk
March day with a tinge of spring in the air, a five-year-
old remarked, "Mrs. Weeks, I don't think Persephone is
with her mother quite yet."

Bruno Bettelhem's *The Uses of Enchantment: The
Meaning and Importance of Fairy Tales*, published in 1976,
also served to support storytelling to children. Though
many readers could not accept Bettelheim's Freudian
interpretations of familiar folk tales, his book persuad-
ed them that the tales were important for children to
hear.

Burton White's research at Harvard in the 60s and
70s confirmed the importance of interaction between children and their caregivers during the first three years of
life. Other researchers, among them Arthur Applebee,
Howard Gardner, and Brian Sutton-Smith, were exploring
the child's sense of stories. Maureen and Hugh Crago,
parents, observed and published their young daughter's
responses to picture books, and Dorothy Butler, grand-
mother of a multi-handicapped child, wrote of the miraculous role books and stories played in Cushla's social and
intellectual development. In response to the growing
evidence that young children were capable of responding
to stories on a sophisticated level, children's librarians began experimenting with "toddler hours," storytelling programs designed for children from eighteen months
to three years old accompanied by a caregiver. The
noticeable lack of story books for toddlers led publishers to bring out attractive board books by talented
authors and illustrators.

In the early 70s storytelling was something most
adults associated with children. Librarians and teachers
had kept the art alive. Then something happened that
resurrected the adult audience for storytelling. Early
in 1973 Jimmy Neil Smith, then a high school teacher and
later a restaurateur and mayor of Jonesborough, Tennessee, was riding in his car when storyteller-comedian

Jerry Clower came on the air. His students' delighted reaction to Clower's monologue started Jimmy thinking about organizing a national storytelling festival. That fall about three hundred people gathered on the lawns of the historic old houses in Jonesborough to swap stories. From that small gathering has grown an annual storytelling festival that attracts thousands of story-telling enthusiasts to this small Appalachian town. Suddenly, grown-ups recognized the value of storytelling for themselves. Perhaps storytelling filled the need for intimacy not easily found in a mobile society or from the electronic storyteller that invaded the family livingroom in the 50s.

In 1974 Jimmy Neil Smith founded the National Association for the Preservation and Perpetuation of Storytelling, better known by its acronym, NAPPS. NAPPS publishes *The National Storytelling Journal*, sponsors an annual storytelling festival during the first weekend of October, an annual conference in June, and a story-telling institute during the summer months. Cousins Connie Regan and Barbara Freeman attended the first national storytelling festival and decided to leave their positions as librarians in Chattanooga, Tennessee, to become travelling storytellers. Since then hundreds of others have left their first profession to join the ranks of professional storytellers, that is, those who make their living solely through storytelling. Probably not since the Middle Ages have there been so many pro-fessional storytellers. They tell in coffee houses, concert halls, churches, museums, parks, and playgrounds, as well as in schools and libraries. Their audiences include adults and children. Their performances are entertainment-oriented.

The shift in modern folklore scholarship from study of the story itself to study of the story within its context served to reinforce the modern teller's focus on performance and the audience's reaction to it. Folk-lorists consider the physical and social environment in which the story is told essential for an understanding of its meaning. The storyteller's voice, gestures, and interaction with the listeners are as important as the story itself.

In 1982 this writer wrote an article reflecting on the effect of storyteller-performers on library story-telling programs. The title of the article, published in *School Library Journal*, is a quote from Mary Gould Davis, Supervisor of Storytelling at the New York Public Library from 1922 to 1933. Miss Davis used to tell her students at Columbia University Library School, "there are no talent scouts in the audience of children," meaning that the story is more important than the teller. In this respect the library storyteller is closer to the traditionist than to the modern professional storyteller. The traditionist tells stories absorbed from a story-telling community; the library storyteller tells from a literary background. It was said of Gudrun Thorne-Thomsen, "when she told a story, it was like watching a tree grow; you felt it coming from such roots!"[8]

Even before the rise of a professional class of storytellers libraries had changed their priorities from story hours for older boys and girls to toddler hours for the very young. Most libraries today offer picture book programs for preschoolers and children in the primary grades. The availability of beautiful picture books and traditional fairy tales in picture book format encourage this practice. Few libraries carry out a regular story hour program for children over eight years of age. The tendency is to invite a professional storyteller to visit the school or public library on a special occasion basis. Guest storytellers have always been a part of the library tradition—one has only to think of Marie Shed-lock, Gudrun Thorne-Thomsen, and Ruth Sawyer. But the library storytelling program was never dependent upon guest tellers. Children need to hear stories on a reg-ular basis. Story hours should not be limited to "special occasions" when a professional teller is avail-able. Research has shown a relationship between hearing stories in childhood and a later love of reading. Recog-nition of the importance of storytelling for children is vital in the fight against illiteracy. To motivate children to read through storytelling requires that the storyteller be proficient in her art. Librarians and teachers who enjoy telling stories to children should be encouraged to do so. Where the staff does not have the inclination or time for this important work, one alter-

native would be to hire "a storyteller-in-residence."
This person should have a wide knowledge of literature
and children's reading interests and a sincere desire
to tell to children. Introducing children to literature
on a daily or weekly basis and encouraging them to participate in the creative act of storytelling require different skills from performing to large audiences. "As
with a traditional audience, children are not passive
listeners, and they have a good ear for the spoken word
since they still live in a predominately oral milieu.
They do not demand a flamboyantly oral/visual performance (though many adults think it necessary). They do
demand sincerity and openness, and they tend to suffer
honest fools gladly. Like a traditional audience they
do not stop to ask, 'Was that profound and meaningful,
or just amusing?' If a story is well-told, they will
absorb other levels of meaning that appeal to their
levels of experience and understanding."[9]

From whichever persuasion one tells--traditionist,
librarian/teacher, or performer--and to whatever age
audience, perhaps there is no better closing than this
thought from Ruth Sawyer: "To be able to create a story,
to make it live during the moment of the telling, to
arouse emotions--wonder, laughter, joy, amazement--this
is the only goal a storyteller may have."[10]

Ellin Greene

REFERENCES

1. Ruth Sawyer, *The Way of the Storyteller* (New York:
    Viking, 1942), p. 46.
2. Anne Pellowski, *The World of Storytelling* (New York:
    Bowker, 1977), p. 14.
3. Anne Carroll Moore, *My Roads to Childhood* (Boston:
    Horn Book, 1961), p. 145.
4. John Cotton Dana, "Storytelling in Libraries."
    Public Libraries 13 (1908), 350.
5. Richard G. Alvey, *The Historical Development of
    Organized Storytelling to Children* (Ann Arbor,
    Mich.: University Microfilms International, 1981),
    p. 16.
6. Ibid., p. 35.
7. Alice Jordan, "Story-telling in Boston." *Horn Book*
    10:3 (May 1934), 182.
8. Frances Clarke Sayers, "A Skimming of Memory." *Horn
    Book* 52:3 (June 1976), 273.
9. Kay Stone, "'To Ease the Heart': Traditional Story-
    telling." *National Storytelling Journal* 1:1 (Winter
    1984), 5.
10. Ruth Sawyer, op. cit., p. 148.

Storytelling

I. BEGINNINGS

"The story," the Bushman prisoner said,
"is like the wind. It comes from a far-
off place and we feel it."

Laurens van der Post
A Story Like the Wind

A. General

1. Colum, Padraic. "Introduction." In *The Complete
   Grimm's Fairy Tales*. New York: Pantheon, 1944, pp.
   vii-xiv.

   In this hypnotic introduction that is as much to
   the world of oral storytelling as to the specific
   Grimm tales, Colum centers on the time and rhythms
   of the folk tradition and how those rhythms of evening tellings were different from the rhythms of
   the working day. At night as stories were told a
   "rhythm that was compulsive, fitted to daily tasks,
   waned, and a rhythm that was acquiescent, fitted
   to wishes, took its place." But when daylight became prolonged by artificial means traditional
   stories began to fade, for the day's rhythm per-
   sisted into night. Though times and places of
   telling folktales may not be the same, the tales
   themselves have maintained their inner truths and
   provide a history that lives within us, that remains more lively than written records, and that
   helps restore our imagination.

2. Colwell, Eileen. "Folk Literature: An Oral Tradition and an Oral Art." *Top of the News* 24 (January 1968): 175-180.

   A succinct historical overview of the storytelling
   tradition in western Europe from its beginnings in
   the telling of some personal exploit in hunting or

war to the development of the hero tale and mythology, the minstrel tradition in the Middle Ages and
its twentieth-century counterpart. This paper was
originally presented in Toronto at the 33rd IFLA
Conference in August 1967. The author, a distinguished British storyteller and librarian, under-
lined the responsibility of modern storytellers to
pass on the "wisdom, beauty and fun" of the ancient
tales.

3. Harrell, John. *Origins and Early Traditions of
    Storytelling*. Kensington, Calif.: York House, 1983.

    The intent of this lively survey of the beginnings
    of storytelling from Cro-Magnon man to Ovid is to
    give modern storytellers a sense of their lineage
    which in turn can give depth to their tellings.
    The modern storyteller must learn as much as possi-
    ble about the story, the meaning it had in the cul-
    ture from which it came, and its meaning for people
    today. Only by so doing can the teller convey its
    spirit to others. Harrell notes the effect of the
    invention of writing on the development of story-
    telling and the tension that continues to exist be-
    tween the oral tradition and the written word.

B. Library Story Hours

4. Beust, Nora E. "The Story Hour: A Significant Pro-
    gram of Children's Departments in Public Libraries."
    School Life 30 (May 1948): 26-28. Reprinted in
    Readings About Children's Literature, by Evelyn R.
    Robinson. New York: McKay, 1966.

    A brief description of story hours in several li-
    braries, including the New York Public Library,
    the Carnegie Library of Pittsburg, and those of

Detroit and Cleveland. Related programs, such as book discussions, puppet shows, radio library story hours, and preschool hours are also mentioned.

5. Blanchard, Alice A. "Story-telling as a Library Tool." In *Library Work with Children*, by Alice I. Hazeltine. New York: Wilson, 1917, pp. 289-295.

In this paper, originally given at a conference at Clark University in 1909, Blanchard, then head of the school department of the Free Public Library of Newark, New Jersey, echoes the sentiments of her director, John Cotton Dana, cautioning against the misuse of storytelling by children's librarians. However, she also gives support for library story-telling if it "advertises the best books, and results in an increased use of them." Stories are to be selected from books on the library shelves and told only to children. Blanchard criticizes children's librarians for spending time preparing their own versions of stories when "they have so much material which they can use at first hand." She is especially critical (and rightly so) of over-simplified versions.

6. Botset, Elizabeth Keith. "The Once-Upon-a-Time Hour." *Carnegie Magazine* 6:9 (February 1933): 266-269.

Botset describes the early story hour program at the Carnegie Library. She credits the origin of library story hours to a Pittsburgh librarian, Charlotte Keith Bissell. Bissell noticed a group of younger children listlessly leafing through picture books. She wondered what the result would be if a librarian *told* stories to such children and why the story hour, so successful in hospitals, had not been tried in libraries to introduce books. The first story hours at Carnegie were for children over nine years of age and the stories told were from Shakespeare and other classics. In 1902

the library began a program for younger children,
"made up of fairy tales, folk literature, and Bible
stories." The program at Carnegie reached its peak
in 1924 when attendance at story hours during the
year numbered nearly 150,000. Botset expresses
regret at the decline in story hours due to the
changing emphasis in library work with children
and reaffirms the values of the library story hour.

7. Children's Librarians' Section. "First Session,
    Bretton Woods Conference." *Bulletin of the American
    Library Association* 3 (1909): 408-420.

    Proceedings of a story hour symposium held on June
    29, 1909, during the ALA Bretton Woods Conference.
    The program consisted of a paper by Gudrun Thorne-
    Thomsen, read by Mr. C.B. Roden, on "The Practical
    Results of Story-Telling in Chicago's Park Reading-
    Rooms," and reports of the storytelling program in
    the New York Public Library, by Annie Carroll Moore;
    the Carnegie Library of Pittsburgh, by Alice I.
    Hazeltine; the Brooklyn Public Library, by Ida J.
    Duff; and the Cleveland Public Library, by Rose
    Gymer. The speakers address the role of storytell-
    ing in the library (and the prerogative of the
    schools in this area), present a picture of library
    story hours at this early date, and offer impressive
    attendance statistics.

8. Dana, John Cotton. "Story-telling in Libraries."
    Public Libraries 13 (1908): 349-351.

    John Cotton Dana held no brief for storytelling in
    libraries, believing it to be the function of the
    schools. "If now, the library by chance has on its
    staff a few altruistic, emotional, dramatic and
    irrepressible child-lovers who do not find ordinary
    library work gives sufficient opportunities for
    altruistic indulgence, and if the library can spare
    them from other work, let it set them at teaching
    the teachers the art of storytelling." His view

represented a minority opinion that is still heard today.

9. Filstrup, Jane Merrill. "The Enchanted Cradle: Early Storytelling in Boston." *Horn Book* 52:6 (December 1976): 601-610.

Recognizing the power of storytelling to captivate children and encourage reading, the Boston Public Library began presenting storytellers at various facilities early in the twentieth century. The project was not only successful, but widely popular, with numbers of up to 1800 listeners per week by 1920. With seventy percent of its population foreign-born or first-generation, Boston was undergoing great cultural integration. And with over ninety percent of the children leaving school by the sixth grade the story hours "reached out to many of these children to supplement amputated school careers." The Boston storytellers believed that extensive exposure to the arts and literature had a critical role in the integrating of so many diverse American heritages.

10. Hardendorff, Jeanne B. "Storytelling and the Story Hour." *Library Trends* 12:1 (July 1963): 52-63.

At the time of the article the library story hour was being questioned from the viewpoint of cost-efficiency. Hardendorff, a storyteller and assistant to the coordinator of work with children at Enoch Pratt Free Library, traces the history of the library story hour and gives the results of a questionnaire she sent to fifty-five children's librarians about its status. Hardendorff makes a clear distinction between "storytelling" and "story hour." By story hour is meant "a regularly scheduled period of activity which includes storytelling or storytelling combined with other activities. In general, and in spite of cutbacks in the number of story hour programs, children's librarians supported the library story hour.

11.   Jordan, Alice M. "Storytelling in Boston 1910-
      1960." *Horn Book* 37 (November 7, 1961): 47-50.

      On the occasion of fifty years of storytelling at
      the Boston Public Library, the first Supervisor
      of Children's Work recalls its beginnings and the
      famous family of tellers, Mary and John Cronan
      and Mrs. Cronan's sister, Margaret W. Powers.

12.   Moore, Anne Carroll. "Report of the Committee on
      Storytelling." *Playground* 4 (August 1910): 162ff.
      Reprinted in *Library Work with Children*, by Alice
      I. Hazeltine. New York: H.W. Wilson, 1917, pp.
      297-315.

      Moore's report gives a picture of the extent to
      which storytelling was being carried out in play-
      grounds, settlement houses, public libraries, and
      other institutions early in the century.

13.   Moore, Anne Carroll. "The Story Hour at Pratt
      Institute Free Library." *Library Journal* 30 (April
      1905): 204-211.

      Moore describes the storytelling program at Pratt,
      considered to be one of the earliest library story-
      telling programs in the country. The story hours
      were held at 7:30 in the evening as many of the
      children worked during the day. They were designed
      for three age groups: four to eight years, eight
      to eleven or twelve, and twelve to sixteen, and
      it was recommended that the group not exceed fifty
      children. Story hours lasted twenty minutes to
      an hour. Moore read aloud or told stories out of
      her own life. Throughout the year there were spe-
      cial days to celebrate, such as the Japanese Chry-
      santhemum Festival in October, Christmas in Decem-
      ber, and Hans Christian Andersen's birthday in
      April. Guest storytellers illustrated their tales
      with colored lantern slides. The article includes
      Moore's philosophy of the library story hour and

her list of essentials for a successful story hour:
(1) a clear definition of purpose and plan,
(2) careful organization of method, (3) the right
person (i.e., storyteller) and (4) the right kind
of group to listen (by age, grade, or special interest).

14. Olcott, Frances Jenkins. "Story-telling--A Public
Library Method." In *Library Work with Children*,
by Alice I. Hazeltine. New York: Wilson, 1917,
pp. 285-288.

A reprint of a paper presented at the National
Child Conference for Research and Welfare held at
Clark University, Worcester, Massachusetts, in
July 1909. Olcott, Director of the Training School
for Children's Librarians and head of children's
work at the Carnegie Library of Pittsburgh, presents storytelling as one of the most effective
ways of introducing large groups of children to
literature. She describes storytelling at the
Carnegie Library, one of the earliest libraries
(perhaps the first) to carry out a systematic program. The story hour cycle extended over an eight-
year period, beginning with nursery tales and end-
ing with stories from Shakespeare. At the end of
the eight years the cycle was repeated. Olcott
asserts that "the library story hour becomes, if
properly utilized, an educational force as well
as a literary guide."

15. Sawyer, Ruth. "Storytelling Fifty Years A-
Growing." In *Reading Without Boundaries*, edited
by Frances Lander Spain. New York: New York Public
Library, 1956, pp. 59-64.

Following a fitting tribute to Washington Irving,
"our first truly American storyteller" and one of
the first trustees of the Astor Library, Sawyer
traces the New York Public Library's fifty-year
heritage of storytelling. Her survey covers Marie

Shedlock's meeting with Anne Carroll Moore, then
librarian at the Pratt Institute and later the
first Supervisor of Work with Children at the Library; the work of Anna Cogswell Tyler, the Library's first Supervisor of Storytelling; Mary
Gould Davis, Miss Cogwell's successor; and Frances
Clarke Sayers. Sawyer notes that the survival of
storytelling as a living art depends on its simplicity and spontaneity. The goal of librarians
is "to bring children, good books and well told
stories into fellowship."

16. "Story-telling Around the World. A Symposium.
     Parts 1-5." *Library Journal* 65 (April 1, 15,
     1940): 285-289; (May 1): 379-381; (June 1): 484-
     487; (July-August): 574-577, 624-627.

A series of five articles by well-known children's
literature specialists. Part I, "The United
States" by Ruth A. Hill, presents the history of
library storytelling from 1899 to the time of the
article and a picture of storytelling activities
in several city systems. Part II, "Europe," by
Blanche Weber, discusses the differences and similarities between library programs in Europe and
the Unites States and covers storytelling activities in France, Holland, Sweden, Norway, Russia,
and England. Part III, "Canada," by Frances W.
Trotter, gives a report of storytelling activities
in the provinces and the children's interest in
their literary heritage from French and English
roots and in Canadian Indian tales. Part IV,
"Hawaii," by Ann McLelland Pfaender and Eloise
West Winstedt, discusses the unique problems of
storytellers working with a conglomerate population
and language differences. Part V, "South America,"
by Hildamar Escalante, covering the influence of the
three distinctive regions of South America on the
creation of stories and folklore, becomes a personal
reminiscence of the writer's childhood experience of
listening to stories.

17. Story-Telling Number. *Horn Book* 10:3 (May 1934): 137-194.

A tribute to Marie Shedlock on the occasion of her birthday. Contents: "Our Fairy Godmother, Marie L. Shedlock," by Anne Carroll Moore; "Letters of tribute to Miss Shedlock"; "The Storyteller's Art," by Mary Gould Davis; "Story-telling in Boston," by Alice M. Jordan; "The Story of a Story-teller," by Margery Bianco; "Storytelling in Ireland," by Padraic Colum. Illustrated with photographs of Shedlock, Mary Gould Davis, Mary Cronan, and other well-known storytellers of the period.

II. PURPOSE AND VALUES OF STORYTELLING

There is also the power of story-telling, and
the whole magic of story-telling, which sus-
tains your life so that you never succumb to
the terrible despair of someone who cannot see
beyond today's happenings. The magic of storytelling lies in the enjoyment of a flight of
language that takes you into another realm.
We enter the realm of poetry or art and discover the pleasure of possessing the skill
to fly.

> Anaïs Nin
> *A Woman Speaks*

18. Alexander, Lloyd. "Identifications and Identi-
     ties." *Wilson Library Bulletin* 45:2 (October
     1970): 144-148.

     In every child's natural search for his identity
     folktales have a great deal to offer, for they let
     the child pretend. "The let's pretend of litera-
     ture can have both an immediate and a long-range
     impact on our lives collectively and individually."
     Each tale takes a child toward part of the basic
     hero story of separation, initiation, and return.
     Each tale allows the child the opportunity to ex-
     plore the deeply emotional and at times non-
     rational levels of being human. Sharing tales
     helps the child find his individuality and at the
     same time helps him find his common bonds with the
     world around him.

19. Anderson, William. "Fairy Tales and the Elementary
     Curriculum or 'The Sleeping Beauty' Reawakened."
     Elementary English 46:5 (May 1969): 563-569.

     While much has been done to explore the psycholog-
     ical complexities of folktales, Anderson feels
     little has been done to fully integrate them into
     the cognitive literature curricula. "Sleeping
     Beauty" is used as an example of how the literary
     side of tales may be explored and shared to help
     the child grow toward an appreciation of adult
     literary conventions. Within tales one can find
     elements of man's relationships to gods, justice,
     and order. Folktales are not childish, but rather
     "representations of the unseen world in exactly
     the way of the Greek gods and goddesses."

20. Applebee, Arthur. "Children and Stories: Learning
     the Rules of the Game." *Language Arts* 56:6 (Sep-
     tember 1979): 641-646.

     The stories children tell grow more complex and
     structured as they mature. At as young an age as
     two and one-half children begin to differentiate
     storytelling as a distinct language function, em-
     ploying narrative conventions and vocal inflec-
     tions. In time, fairy tale characters become a
     type of literary shorthand for complex elements
     as children work to match the quality of the sto-
     ries they are told. Tales allow the child to re-
     flect on his world and provide safe opportunities
     via structure for exploring disturbing or threaten-
     ing ideas. Just as in the rules of a game it is
     vital for the child to learn the limits, what can
     and cannot be part of the narrative, for "part of
     the usefulness of stories is that through them we
     can explore those limits without losing the game."

21. Arewa, E. Ojo. "The Style and Technique of Actual
     Dramatic Process of Narration Among the School
     Children of a Nigerian Group." *Fabula* 15 (1974):
     47-52.

     Drawing from experience both as child and teacher,
     Arewa discusses the Nigerian child's relationships
     to story both as listener and teller. While not
     the skillful tellers they hear at community ses-
     sions, the children employ the same range of styl-
     ing as adults. Nonverbal or facial mimicry is
     used effectively as are onomatopoetic expressions
     that connote sounds (i.e., a running horse: ku tu
     pa ku tu pa). Repetition is also frequently em-
     ployed in the form of reoccurring songs, phrases,
     and actions which aid the child teller in creating
     dramatic urgency. With the children viewing story-
     telling as a joint enterprise between narrator and
     audience, fear of performing for peers is all but
     absent as the teller takes the role as leader and
     the listening children act as supporters for the

teller. "The inclusion of story-telling as a part of the curriculum in the lower grades of the elementary school in Nigeria is a good index of the importance attached to story-telling, not only as a source of enjoyment in both the traditional and modern situations, but as a way of maintaining a continuity between the two spheres of life."

22. Auden, W.H. "Grimm and Andersen." In *Forewords and Afterwords*. New York: Random House, 1973, pp. 198-208.

Believing the fairy tale to be a dramatic and symbolic projection of the psyche, Auden supports the sharing of folktales. Tales are vital to contemporary children by the mere fact that they are enjoyed. Tales told may indeed on occasion frighten a child, but usually only in cases where the story is told only once. Repetition is the key with each telling of the story, allowing the child to experience new emotions and master his initial fears. And to the complaints that tales present a false view of reality Auden responds: "No fairy story ever claimed to be a description of the external world and no sane child has ever believed it was." In examining the Grimm tale "The Water of Life" and various Andersen stories, Auden discusses the differences in folktales and literary tales--one emphasizing plot, the other character-- and what each may provide the listener and reader.

23. Bellon, Elner C. "Language Development Through Storytelling Activities." *School Library Media Quarterly* 3:2 (Winter 1975): 149-156.

Bellon cites recent research supportive of storytelling as a language development activity. Picture books and storytelling introduce children to a rich vocabulary and complex language structure, offer opportunities to use language through discussion or creative drama following the story,

and personalize literature and communication. Use
of flannelgraphs, transparencies, and puppets are
suggested as "incentives" for speech and communication.

24.   Bettelheim, Bruno. *The Uses of Enchantment: The
      Meaning and Importance of Fairy Tales*. New York:
      Knopf, 1976.

      Bettelheim's discussion of fairy tales and their
      valuable place in our lives is thought provoking
      and has done much to recharge popular interest in
      oral storytelling. Of special interest are chap-
      ters entitled "Fear of Fantasy: Why Were Fairy
      Tales Outlawed?" and "Fantasy, Recovery, Escape
      and Consolation: On the Telling of Fairy Stories."
      Bettelheim believes the teller's feelings toward
      the tale are a crucial element in the tale's suc-
      cess in reaching the child. "The adult's sense
      of active participation in telling the story makes
      a vital contribution to, and greatly enriches,
      the child's experience of it. It entails an af-
      firmation of his personality through a particular
      shared experience with another human being." While
      not all readers will find themselves in full agree-
      ment with Bettelheim's final chapters applying
      Freudian analysis to specific tales, they do pro-
      vide a challenging perspective which can be com-
      pared with other interpretations. The core of
      this book first appeared as "Reflections" in *The
      New Yorker,* December 8, 1975.

25.   Chukovsky, Kornei. "The Battle for the Fairy
      Tale." In *From Two to Five*, translated by Miriam
      Morton. Berkeley: University of California Press,
      1963, pp. 114-139.

      A leading supporter of fairy tales for children
      in the U.S.S.R., Chukovsky discusses the many val-
      ues of sharing tales as art and as food for the
      spirit. Fairy tales help children find their place

in the world and allow them to live a wide variety of emotional experiences. Tales shared work
to "awaken, nurture, and strengthen in the responsive soul of the child this invaluable ability to feel compassion for another's unhappiness
and to share in another's happiness--without this
man is inhuman." In addition, fairy tales foster
the imagination so necessary for future scientists
and scholars as well as poets, and as such, fill
a vital need in children's lives. This essay has
also been reprinted in *Children and Literature:
Views and Reviews*, edited by Virginia Haviland
(Glenview, Ill.: Scott Foresman, 1973). It was
first published in Russian in 1929.

26. Coles, Robert. "Children's Stories: The Link to
a Past." In *Children's Literature*. Vol. 8. New
Haven, Conn.: Yale University Press, 1980, pp.
141-146.

The noted child psychiatrist writes about children's "natural" development of narrative interest
and its purpose in their lives. "Stories connect
children to the past of their parents, their people; stories also enable children to connect themselves to something even more fundamental, their
very essence as talking, listening, thinking crea-
tures, who are anxious to fit together, as best
they are able, whatever they learn about human
experience."

27. Colum, Padraic. *Storytelling: New and Old*. New
York: Macmillan, 1961.

Remembering the stories and storytellers he heard
as a child, Colum discusses the similarities and
differences to contemporary storytelling sessions.
Above all the storyteller must have respect for
the child's mind and tell the story in a direct
and kindly manner. The best tellers are those
"who seem to be giving us in the stories they are

telling fragments of their reverie" and sharing
spontaneity as if they have just discovered something going on. Beyond their innate joy, tales
also aid the child in making himself at home in
his world of imagination, intuition, and reality.
And with stories nurturing the imagination, desire
for what is imagined grows, in time, to the point
of creating what once was only a dream. This essay
first appeared in Padraic Colum's *The Fountain of
Youth* published by Macmillan in 1927.

28.   Duff, Annis. "A Brief for Fairy Tales." In *Be-
      quest of Wings*. New York: Viking, 1956, pp. 170-
      180.

      A former bookshop owner and children's book editor
      presents her arguments in favor of fairy tales
      for children. Duff replies to common objections:
      violence, tragedy, and death in fairy tales, be-
      havior that is contrary to ethical principles,
      and escape from reality. "My impression is that
      people in fairy tales behave pretty much as people
      do in real life.... There are strong and weak
      people, people with great intelligence, and many
      with little or none. And in fairy tales, each
      type, with the action that represents it, is
      brought to life objectively, emphatically and con-
      sistently." Duff's commonsensical approach is
      illustrated with frequent references to her young
      daughter's reactions to the tales.

29.   Ekrem, Selma. "What Fairy Tales Meant to a Turkish
      Child." *Horn Book* 17:2 (March-April 1941): 122-
      126.

      Ekrem writes a warm reminiscence of her childhood
      in Turkey where she had a nurse who was a master
      of household storytelling sessions. From such
      early storytelling experiences Ekrem grew to love
      imaginative tales and eagerly learned to read
      French and English for there were no children's

books in Turkish at the time. Though tales were
rarely written down due to social attitudes, they
were shared endlessly for storytelling was "an
ancient and honored profession and one of the few
open to Turkish women in the past" and regarded
as an art form of great value and vitality.

30. Engler, Martha C. "Message Versus Machine: The
     Art of the Storyteller." *Catholic Library World*
     44 (1973) 471-477.

A stirring call for storytellers to counterbalance
the dehumanizing effects of the new technology
which Marshall McLuhan warned against in his book,
Understanding Media. To keep children from becoming "the percussed victims of the new technology"
Engler recommends telling them folktales, myths,
legends and hero tales, literary fairy tales, especially those by Hans Christian Andersen, and
stories from the Bible. She pays tribute to six
inspiring storytellers of the twentieth century:
Marie Shedlock, Ruth Sawyer, Seumas MacManus, John
and Mary Cronan, and Frances Clarke Sayers.

31. Favat, F. Andre. *Child and Tale: The Origins of
     Interest*. Urbana, Ill.: National Council of Teach-
     ers of English, 1977.

Using a literary reservoir (the tales of Perrault,
Grimm, and Andersen) and a psychological reservoir
(Piaget, Freud, Jung) Favat attempts to discover
the reasons for children's interest in fairy tales.
He concludes that peak interest occurs between
ages six and eight because the fairy tale corres-
ponds with the child's conception of the world at
that age. There is a correspondence between the
construction of the fairy tale and the child's
belief in magic, animism, morality, causality,
and egocentrism. Favat exhorts his colleagues to
test his methodology in other areas of children's
reading interests. Professionals would then be

able to answer such questions as "What is it about
this particular book that would cause children of
what age and psychological disposition to respond
to it in what ways?" or, conversely, "What is it
about children of this particular age and psychological disposition that would cause them to respond to what books in what ways?" Favat notes
"Children are interested in certain types of reading at certain stages in their development because
they fulfill the needs and desires children have
at these stages." Favat's doctoral study provides
a workable construct "to prove" what teachers and
librarians have intuited all along.

32. Garthwaite, Marion. "The Acid Test." *Horn Book*
     39:4 (August 1963): 408-411.

     "Witches should be sour, like good lemons, and as
     tart and zestful." Children find emotional release
     in folktales about witches and ogres who are justly
     punished for their villanous deeds. Such tales
     should be told "with tongue in cheek, twinkle in
     eye, laughter in heart." Watered-down versions
     should be avoided by the storyteller--children do
     not find them satisfying.

33. Green, George H. *Psychoanalysis in the Classroom.*
     New York: Putnam, 1922, pp. 65-67; 214-218.

     The child is drawn to the fairy tale for its world
     of intensity and because it is also the world the
     child sees himself in. Children project themselves
     into the tales' heroes and find responses to many
     of their instinctive wishes and hopes for the fu-
     ture. "Children are absorbed in fairy tales as
     they are not absorbed in their lessons [and] we
     seem forced to conclude that what interests us
     most is ourselves, and that the extent of our in-
     terest in something else depends upon the extent
     to which we are able to identify ourselves with
     it." Fairy tales reflect the child's life and

also take him beyond the struggles to happily re-
solved conclusions.

34. Greene, Ellin. "There Are No Talent Scouts...."
    School Library Journal 29:3 (November 1982): 25-27.

    Mary Gould Davis, a fine teacher of storytelling,
    used to tell her students, "There are no talent
    scouts in the audience of children," meaning that
    the story was more important than the teller. In
    this article a contemporary teacher of storytelling
    expresses her concerns about the effect of "story-
    teller-performers" on the library's program. Chil-
    dren need to hear stories on a regular basis, not
    only when a "star-teller" is available. Greene
    reaffirms the library's primary purpose for story-
    telling: to introduce children to literary pleasure
    and encourage reading. The librarian's strength
    lies in her broad knowledge of the literature,
    expertise in selection, and commitment to sharing
    literature with children.

35. Haley, Gail E. "Caldecott Award Acceptance." *Horn
    Book* 47 (1971): 363-368.

    In her Caldecott acceptance speech for *A Story—
    A Story*, Haley made an eloquent statement about
    the relationship between hearing stories in child-
    hood and becoming a reader. In part she said:
    "Deprive a child of love and he will reach for
    affection or clamor for attention at the expense
    of other aspirations. Deprive him of fantasy and
    he may try, on his own, to make up even for that
    deficit. But children who are not spoken to by
    live and responsive adults will not learn to speak
    properly. Children who are not answered will stop
    asking questions. They will become incurious.
    And children who are not told stories and who are
    not read to will have few reasons for wanting to
    learn to read."

36. Hartmann, Waltraut. "Identification and Projection
     in Folk Fairy-Tales and in Fantastic Stories for
     Children." *Bookbird* 7:2 (1969): 8-17.

     The developing child readily identifies with fairy
     tale heroes because the heroes are developing and
     struggling as is the child. Finding such psycho-
     logical friends in stories, the child, at the same
     time he begins to imitate the hero's attitudes,
     starts to understand the story in greater degree.
     The child's love of folktale heroes is not just
     admiration, but a pleasure in self-discovery as
     well.

37. Haviland, Virginia. "Fairy Tales and Creativity."
     In *How Can Children's Literature Meet the Needs
     of Modern Children: Fairy Tales and Poetry Today*.
     Munich: Arbeitskreis für Jugendliteratur V, 1977,
     pp. 56-61.

     The former Chief of Children's Services at the
     Library of Congress cites a number of scientists
     and writers, among them Albert Einstein, John
     Tindale, Charles Dickens, Hans Christian Andersen,
     Walter de la Mare, Eleanor Farjeon, and Joan Aiken,
     who professed that hearing imaginative literature
     in childhood influenced their development as cre-
     ative adults. Adults need to keep imaginative
     literature alive for children through the art of
     storytelling. This paper was presented at the
     Fifteenth Congress of the International Board of
     Books for Young People (IBBY) held at the Padios
     of Political and Economic Studies in Athens, Sep-
     tember 28-October 2, 1976.

38. Hazard, Paul. "Fairy Tales and Their Meaning."
     In *Books Children and Men*. Boston: Horn Book,
     1944, pp. 157-161.

     Hazard's essay is a brief but vibrant look at the
     place folktales have in our lives and how they

link us to the human past and allow each child to
begin anew the journey of the human spirit. Stories have traveled and evolved as people have,
and have been especially treasured by children.
"Once upon a time, formerly, at a period so far
removed from us that we are unable to visualize
it to ourselves, there was the very same story"
and it will live on as long as there are people
to tell it and children to listen.

39. Heath, Shirley Brice. *Ways with Words: Language,*
Life and Work in Communities and Classrooms. New
York: Cambridge University Press, 1983.

Heath is an anthropologist and former English
teacher whose unique social research recently won
her the David Russell Award. She writes with respect for diverse cultures and the many ways of
knowing, doing, and being, including storytelling.

40. Heisig, James W. "Bruno Bettelheim and the Fairy
Tales." *Children's Literature* 6 (1977): 93-114.

In this critical reading of Bettelheim's *The Uses*
of Enchantment Heisig suggests that fairy tales
may be more open-ended than Bettelheim's psycho-
analytic approach permits. One could say: "You
have invested enough time and imagination in wrest-
ing with their meaning only when you finally come
to tell the stories yourself, just as they are,
without embarrassment, and to allow them to sleep
quietly in your heart." Adults as well as children
can find wisdom in fairy tales.

41. Heuscher, Julius E. *A Psychiatric Study of Myths*
and Fairy Tales: Their Origin, Meaning and Useful-
ness. Springfield, Ill.: Thomas, 1974.

Seeing no sharp boundaries between the therapeutic
and growth enhancing elements of folklore, Heuscher

explores a variety of related issues ranging from
the concern about the possible negative influence
of tales to their symbolic language. Heuscher is
eclectic in his approach, always working with the
central theory in mind that the truth of the fairy
tale is "not simply objectively given, but depends
upon the ability of the listener to *perceive* the
truth." This is extended to the adult reader or
teller who, having a respect and understanding of
a tale, is better able to share it and its hidden
meanings with the child. Chapters of special interest to storytellers are: "A Critique of Some
Interpretations of Myths and Fairy Tales"; "The
Language of Fairy Tales and Myth"; "The Significance Given to Fairy Tales and Myths in Our Times";
and "Folklore in Education."

42.   Hornyansky, Michael. "The Truth of Fables." In
      Only Connect: Readings on Children's Literature,
      edited by Sheila Egoff. New York: Oxford Univer-
      sity Press, 1969, pp. 121-132.

      Fairy tales have staying power even for the modern
      child addicted to television and the comics. This
      is so because "they are good solid myths based in
      the child's own world and told directly, without
      archness or sentimentality or other adult non-
      sense." Hornyansky challenges Disney and others
      who tamper with such tales. His Freudian inter-
      pretations of "Snow-White," "Hansel and Gretel,"
      and "Jack and the Beanstalk" are saved from
      Bettelheim's heaviness by charming anecdotes about
      the responses of the author's children to the
      tales. This essay was first published in *The
      Tamarack Review*, August 1965.

43. Hughes, Ted. "Myth and Education." In *Writers, Critics and Children,* edited by Geoff Fox and others. New York: Agathon Press, 1976, pp. 77-94.

Knowing that first lessons and experiences can be the most important ones, Hughes explores the place of story in imagination and the power of story to create powerful images and reservoirs of meaning. To know a story is a kind of wealth and one that helps the child begin to find a balance between the inner and outer worlds of his body which are "intricately interdependent at every moment." Drawing from Plato, Hughes believes all traditional stories are part of his educational syllabus and that small tales can be just as vigorous in terms of education as major myths. "A simple tale, told at the right moment, transforms a person's life with the order its pattern brings to incoherent energies." Each tale is an inseparable combination of pattern and images that can provide new perceptions of feeling and spirit that might have remained dormant if the tale hadn't been experienced. An earlier and slightly different version of this essay was printed in *Children's Literature in Education* in March 1970.

44. Johnson, N.M. "Shelter Stories." *Junior Bookshelf* 6 (July 1942): 45-48.

With all of England under stress during World War II Johnson found folktales a special thing to share and especially appropriate, for they were known to the children and served as supportive friends while their immediate world was filled with bombs and darkness. Hoping to ease their fears and provide more pleasant thoughts for dreams, Johnson told tales such as "Cinderella" and "Hansel and Gretel" in which right may struggle, but always conquers might.

45. Lasser, Michael. "The Story World." *Journal of
     Reading* 20:6 (March 1977): 456-465.

     Developing his thesis that tales "are the imagina-
     tion's humanizing gift to us all," Lasser explores
     the literary and emotional connections between
     children and stories. On the literal level tales
     offer children enhancement through their quality
     of writing. Tales' wider use of language, inner
     continuity, and close relationship to myth afford
     the child greater depths and enjoyment in his read-
     ing into and through adulthood. Stories speak
     directly to the child in vivid images and often
     startling metaphors that offer hope and reassur-
     ance, a reassurance that brings insight even when
     filled with laughter. While tales may be nonsense,
     they are never senseless. Rooted solidly in our
     past and the truths of intuition, tales "may well
     be our children's brightest chance for a future
     marked by clarity, imagination and hope."

46. Leeper, Faye. "Talking and Touching: A Function
     of Storytelling." In *Paisanos: A Folklore Miscel-
     lany,* edited by Francis Edward Abernethy. Austin:
     The Encino Press, 1978, pp. 137-146.

     Utilizing research on touching and body language,
     Leeper discusses the physical elements of story-
     telling in informal situations where even gestures
     and facial expressions indicate a physical aware-
     ness between teller and listener. As people age
     and mature their non-sexual touching decreases,
     yet the sharing of stories and jokes brings about
     back slapping, lap sitting, arms over shoulders,
     and relaxed interactions. Where stroking with
     words has replaced hands, Leeper finds storytelling
     "still the most ideally socially acceptable [means]
     ... for consumating the desire for being close to
     other human beings."

47. Le Guin, Ursula. "The Child and the Shadow." In
    *The Language of the Night: Essays on Fantasy and
    Science Fiction*, edited by Susan Wood. New York:
    Putnam, 1979, pp. 59-71.

    Far from being escapism, fantasy and tales for
    children offer greater accessibility to inner
    truths for fantasy is the natural language "for
    the recounting of the spiritual journey and the
    struggle of good and evil in the soul." Fantasy
    as a genre is able to avoid the pitfalls of real-
    istic fiction's stress on issues and stereotypes
    and explores through archetypes and symbolism the
    collective consciousness shared by all individuals.
    Discussing Andersen's "The Man Without a Shadow"
    Le Guin explores the way tales may help the child
    come to face his own shadow and his inner self,
    thus growing toward self-knowledge and wholeness.

48. L'Engle, Madeleine. "What Is Real?" *Language
    Arts* 55:4 (April 1978): 447-451.

    "... the fairy tale world is ... the world of the
    whole person, where we aren't limited to our in-
    tellect at the sacrifice of our intuition."
    L'Engle relates five elements of the fairy tale:
    the Quest, the Younger Son, the Wise Princess,
    the talking beast and the monsters, and the happy
    ending, to our personal lives. It is through the
    fairy tale that we begin to understand the reality
    of ourselves and others.

49. Lewis, Claudia. "Fairy Tales and Fantasy in the
    Classroom." *Childhood Education* 49:2 (November
    1972): 64-67.

    A report of an experiment in which four classroom
    teachers used six books (chosen from a list of
    sixteen) with their students in kindergarten,
    grades 2, 4, and 6. Related activities were car-
    ried out, including creative movement, drama,

story-writing, role-playing, puppetry, painting,
and music interpretation. Their responses indi-
cated that fairy tales and fantasy mirror the children's concerns and can enrich their experience
in living.

50.   Lurie, Alison. "Fairy Tale Liberation." *New York
       Times Review of Books*, December 17, 1970, p. 42.

       Lurie discusses the "here and now" stories of Lucy
       Sprague Mitchell and basal readers as being not
       only more boring than daily life, but also far
       from reality. "The fairy tales had been right all
       along" she discovered at maturity, "the world was
       full of hostile, stupid giants and perilous castles
       and people who abandoned their children in the
       nearest forest." Fairy tales were also far ahead
       in regard to women's liberation, for in tales male
       protagonists are equalled in number by clever
       daughters, fairy godmothers, and wise women and
       villians by witches and stepmothers. This has
       been reprinted in *Sharing Literature With Chil-
       dren: A Thematic Approach,* edited by Francelia
       Butler (New York: McKay, 1977).

51.   Melani, Lilia. "A Child's Psyche: Recollections
       of Fairy Tales, Myths and Romances." *The Lion
       and the Unicorn* 3 (1979): 14-27.

       Drawing heavily from personal experiences with
       stories, some frightening (Andersen) and others
       warming, Melani explores the child's often intense
       and always special involvement with tales. For
       each child the "special" tale will be different,
       but once found it will be read and reread, and
       asked for again, for it gives strength and comfort
       to the child, and in turn opens his world to wider
       experiences. The connection of child and tale is
       so rich that there can be no reason not to share
       many tales in search for the one "special" one.

52. Mumford, Lewis. "Fact and Fantasy." In *Green
     Memories: The Story of Geddes Mumford*. New York:
     Harcourt, 1947. Reprinted Westport, Conn.: Green-
     wood Press, 1973, pp. 62-67.

     This is a father's warm and reflective recollection
     of his son's childhood during the 1920s and 1930s
     and the stories he heard. Raised in the period
     of "here and now" factual literature, Mumford's
     son had no overt interest in myths and tales, but
     at the same time was involved in the deep primeval
     world of his unconscious and created surrealistic
     daydreams. Whether or not he heard stories, the
     boy created his own. Mumford wonders if efforts
     to protect him by ignoring folktales was wise after
     all, concluding "We did not get rid of the Drag-
     on[;] we only banished St. George."

53. Nesbitt, Elizabeth. "Hold to That Which Is Good."
     Horn Book 16:1 (January-February 1940): 7-15.

     A talk presented at a preconference of the American
     Library Association held in San Francisco in June
     1939. Emphasis in library work with children was
     shifting from reading for literary pleasure to
     reading for information and time spent preparing
     story hours was questioned. Nesbitt, then Asso-
     ciate Professor of Library Science at Carnegie
     Library School, made an eloquent plea for continu-
     ation of the library story hour and the importance
     of the storyteller as an interpreter of literature
     for the child.

54. Newland, Mary Reed. "Storytelling." *Catholic
     Library World* 45:1 (July-August 1973): 31-33.

     More a pep-talk than a "how to" article, Newland
     provides reasons for sharing stories and sees it
     as a "child's first experience of live theater
     [that takes] precedence over every other form of
     entertainment, even television." The effects of

storytelling are long lasting and Newland, a storyteller herself, recounts incidents of adults she
met who warmly remembered stories she had told
them years before. They remembered in part because
the stories were told with joy and care of selection. And also because the teller gave them the
story as a gift and allowed them to find the moral
message in their own time and own way, thus leaving
them something to treasure all their own.

55.   Sayers, Frances Clarke. "From Me to You." In
      Summoned by Books. New York: Viking, 1965, pp.
      95-98.

      The quality of confiding intimacy is one of the
      storyteller's greatest gifts. Even in a visual
      age the voice and the words of the storyteller
      have power, for "the storyteller deals with the
      stuff of the spirit." This inspiring essay from
      a gifted librarian-storyteller originally appeared
      in *Library Journal*, 15 September 1956.

56.   Schachtel, Ernest G. "The Child and the Story."
      In *Metamorphosis*. New York: Basic Books, 1959,
      pp. 239-265.

      Young children often insist on hearing the same
      story over and over again without any changes
      in the text. Schachtel believes that to the
      child the story is an object that must be grasped
      and digested gradually so repeated hearings are
      needed. To have it change even slightly would
      make his task of assimilation frustrating and more
      complicated. The child is actively learning the
      differences among reality, representations of re-
      ality, possibility, and pure fantasy. It is the
      same experience the adult has with a painting to
      which he returns time and again, with each new
      encounter revealing new elements. "Before the
      child can read, the only way to be sure that he
      can rely on a story is by having it reread or

retold to him and making quite sure that it is
really the same story." Schachtel also reminds
one that the preoccupation with reading only the
latest stories (as if the importance is to consume
them rather than interact with them) is peculiar
to our current time and culture, while repeated
readings and hearings of stories are quite common
elsewhere and desired by adults.

57. Scherf, Walter. "Family Conflicts and Emancipation in Fairy Tales." *Children's Literature* 3
(1975): 77-93.

Scherf studied 176 traditional folktales and found
that 169 of them reflected family conflict: son-
father, daughter-father, son-mother, daughter-
mother. He concluded that the function of these
so-called magic tales is to help the child "break
away from the old family relations and to lead to
real emancipation and adulthood."

58. Shannon, George. "Shared Treasures: Folktales,
Joy and the Listening Child as Artist." *National
Storytelling Journal* 1:3 (Summer 1984): 3-6.

Exploring the inner relationship of child to folktale Shannon believes listening to be an artistic
as well as joyful experience. As the tale is told
the child creatively interacts with the tale's
archetypes, images, and rhythms to make with the
teller a unique and personal experience. As in
all arts, the child's making of art becomes a making and defining of self. It is this act of creation and discovery that brings about the deepest
sense of joy in regard to folktales and storytelling. Child and tale, teller and child are
interwoven in an absorbing time of giving, and
one that for the child becomes his first encounter
with artistic and spiritual oneness and forms a
strong beginning toward a life of wonder and belief.

59.   Shannon, George. "Storytelling and the Schools."
      English Journal 68:5 (May 1979): 50-51.

      The oldest of literatures and textbooks, folktales
      can be thoughtfully integrated into all areas of
      the school curriculum. That the integration be
      done with care and intelligence is important, for
      didactic use will destroy the folktale's artistic
      values as excellent literature. While always en-
      tertaining, folktales also bring human emotions
      to social studies, powers of imagination to
      science, a finer ear to literature, an increased
      eye for imagery, and within all of these, a strong
      sense of morality as well.

60.   Sherman, John Lee. "Storytelling with Young Chil-
      dren." *Young Children* 34:1 (January 1979): 20-27.

      Believing that the roots of all other narrative
      art forms are present in storytelling, Sherman
      discusses the rewards and pleasures for both child
      and teacher in telling stories in various forms.
      "Just as it was humanity's first narrative art,
      so should it be each individual's." Children who
      are told stories also begin to tell more stories
      on their own. Whether traditional, personal ex-
      perience, or personal imagination stories, having
      a true enthusiasm for the tale and the telling
      does a great deal to insure success. Sherman
      briefly discusses voice and technique, but speaks
      primarily of the benefits of storytelling for the
      child as it offers new experiences, life-sustaining
      myths, values, pleasures, and symbolic interpre-
      tations of existence.

61.   Simmons, Leo W. *The Role of the Aged in Primitive
      Society*. New Haven: Yale University Press, 1945,
      pp. 99-102.

      Cultures as distant as the Crow and Xosa form pat-
      terns of elders passing on social education to

children through the telling of stories. In addition to the entertaining story sessions a tale is
often told to reinforce the teaching after a child
has been corrected. Beyond the value of the content shared, such storytelling by elders gives
them a vital role within their culture once they
are physically less able and develops strong ties
among the generations and in families.

62. Smardo, Frances A., and Curry, John F. *What Research Tells Us About Storyhours and Receptive
Language*. Dallas: Dallas Public Library, 1982.

A report of a study designed to compare the effec-
tiveness of three types of story hour presentations
on the receptive language of preschool children
of varying socioeconomic levels. The three types
of story hour presentations were "live," videotape,
and 16mm film. Receptive language is defined as
the ability to understand language which is heard.
The study was carried out by the head of Early
Childhood Services at the Dallas Public Library
and a professor at North Texas State University
with children enrolled in child care centers in
Dallas. "Live" storytelling was found to be more
effective than either film or video presentations.
The authors cite related research and emphasize
the need for further investigation.

63. Spagnoli, Cathy. "A Storyteller's India." *National Storytelling Journal* 1:2 (Spring 1984): 3-
6.

First encountering Indian stories when she was
critically ill and partially nursed back to health
with stories, Spagnoli relates the vividness and
variety of storytelling in India. Stories do much
to preserve Indian history and have helped influence people during times of social reform, for
they are told everywhere and in many ways. Many
tales and styles of telling are dying with the

elders, however, for no one is taking their place
and thus pieces of Indian heritage are beginning
to fade. Still, all in all, storytelling is strong
in India, with tales being told in schools, houses,
streets, by mountain streams, as well as via mother's lips. Dramas, tales, and puppet plays of
folk literature continue to preserve the stories
India has long protected from various foreign influences and challenges.

64.   Studer, Norman. "The Place of Folklore in Education." *New York Folklore Quarterly* 18:1 (Spring
1962): 3-12.

In a world where everyone is mobile and the ability
to develop a sense of continuity is more and more
difficult, Studer believes the study of folk literature may offer bridges to people's culture and
family heritage. Folk literature in the curriculum serves to build the student's sense of self
and of how he relates to the human world around
him. One of the first creative arts, folk tales
continue to enrich those who tell and share them.

65.   Travers, P.L. "Grimm's Women" (The Guest Word).
New York Times Book Review, November 16, 1975, p.
59.

Tongue in cheek, Travers turns to Grimm in reply
to a young woman's question, "How can I learn to
be a woman?" She presents several Grimm heroines--
Cinderella, Little Two-Eyes, the Fisherman's Wife,
et al.--one of whom a woman might, or might not,
wish to take as a role model. Travers' point, of
course, is that Grimm's women are not passive as
commonly supposed, but varied, wise, and powerful.

66. Travers, P.L. "Only Connect." In *Only Connect: Readings on Children's Literature,* edited by Sheila Egoff, New York: Oxford University Press, 1969.

    Travers discusses fairy tales and their continual influence on her person and work. Fairy tales come, she believes, straight from myth and not one person or group has yet been able to exhaust their meaning; like a magic purse, every time one thinks he's found the last coin there is suddenly another one. Since fairy tales are connected with myth, they are not just entertainment for children. Travers believes that if one must disembowel a tale in order to tell it to children, it shouldn't be told. By examining her own favorite childhood tales, Travers concludes that tales are not frightening to children, but rather are filled with difficult truths, that when shared, enable the child to connect, however he needs, with other ideas and feelings.

67. Tucker, Nicholas. "Fairy Stories, Myths and Legends." In *The Child and the Book: A Psychological and Literary Exploration.* Cambridge: Cambridge University Press, 1981, pp. 67-96.

    Though Tucker addresses his discussion to the child's reading of folktales, it applies with equal value to the telling and the listening to them. Beginning with a brief overview of past theories on the effect of tales on children by Montessori, Chesterton, Chukovsky, Piaget, Bettelheim, and Jones, Tucker goes on to compare and contrast Freudian and Jungian approaches to specific tales, establishing that even within one approach there will not be uniformity. "Psychoanalytic interpretations of fairy tales are often ingenious, but mutually inconsistent. All such interpretations--especially when they claim to be exclusive--should be treated with caution, but to rule them out altogether would be to abandon the only type of explanation which has gone anywhere near accounting for the world-wide popularity of fairy-tales."

68.   Viguers, Ruth Hill. "Over the Drawbridge and into
the Castle." *Horn Book* 27:1 (January 1951): 54-
62.

An inspiring article by a children's librarian of
international repute about the values of storytelling in developing imagination. Viguers includes poetry and song in storytelling as part of
the child's introduction to literature.

69.   Winkler, Franz. "Information and Education." In
Man, the Bridge Between Two Worlds. New York:
Harper, 1960, pp. 205-215.

Although a child may remember a subject taught
through television it will remain a separate element, for he has not struggled internally with
the information. The folktale when told, however,
does the opposite, by actively involving the
child's mind and spirit. "When we tell a fairy
tale to a child," states Winkler, "we must never
forget that it deals primarily with man's ... soul
life [and] is capable of speaking directly to the
child's innate understanding." Tales are powerful,
but should not be disarmed through editing or rewriting, for their power stems from their natural
metaphoric richness and offers no threat when carefully selected with regard to situation and per-
sonalities of listeners.

70.   Wolkstein, Diane, and Jordon-Smith, Paul. "Telling
Stories: A Conversation." *Parabola* 2:4 (1978):
82-91.

In this conversation between two storyteller-
writers the emotional and aesthetic worlds of story
are explored. Rather than worrying about the psychological interpretations, Wolkstein believes "a
better place to start is how *you* understand it
and what happens to *you* when you hear a story and
to know, really, what is being given to you."

Stories are entertaining yet in a poetic form that
is both gripping and beautiful, with their emotional and aesthetic elements working in tandem.
Their emotional truths are shared covertly in the
telling, making the manner of telling of true importance. One must listen and tell with intellect
and heart because a part of storytelling is the
non-interruption. In storytelling you enter a
world, go through its struggles, and leave, but
if the tale is interrupted or stopped the tale
can't solve its struggle and the listener is left
frustrated. Stories told completely, both when
the teller IS the tale and from beginning to end,
allow the listeners to be a part of the story and
explore new worlds with the storyteller.

71. Wood, Grace. "What Lies Behind Fairy Tales."
    Contemporary Review 185 (June 1954): 364-367.

    In fairy tales, which Wood sees as primarily adult
    tales, the child "sees his own situation ... and
    sees himself by enchantment as conqueror" as he
    deals with metaphoric dragons, witches, and forests
    in which he could lose his way. Like dreams, fairy
    tales have different meanings at different levels,
    ranging from occurrences in daily life to the con-
    sideration of the spiritual world. To demonstrate
    the vitality and enchantment of tales in which the
    protagonist rarely succeeds without some form of
    magical help and/or sensitivity Wood provides brief
    analyses of "Sleeping Beauty" and other tales.

72. Yolen, Jane. *Touch Magic: Fantasy, Faerie and
    Folklore in the Literature of Childhood*. New
    York: Philomel, 1981.

    Ten lively essays on the importance of fairy tales
    and fantasy in the child's social, emotional, and
    intellectual development. Such literature helps
    children develop their imagination and acquire a
    rich language. Yolen believes in the magic of

story. Her own fairy tales which draw on traditional material have become modern classics. Portions of these essays appeared in slightly altered
form in magazines such as *Horn Book, Children's
Literature in Education,* and *Parabola.*

III. ART AND TECHNIQUE OF STORYTELLING

She told her tales in a quiet, mysterious
voice, her face close to mine, gazing into
my eyes with dilated pupils as though she
were pouring into my heart a stream of
strength to support. She sang, rather than
spoke, and the further she went, the more
rhythmic became her style. It was an inex-
pressible joy to listen to her, and when she
had finished a tale I would cry: "Go on!"

Maxim Gorky
My Childhood

73. Ager, Lynn Price. "Storyknifing: An Alaskan Eskimo
    Girls' Game." *Journal of the Folklore Institute*
    11:3 (1975): 187-198.

    Long before children's picturebooks were created
    young female Eskimos (Yuk) in southwestern Alaska
    were illustrating tales as they told them.
    Using carved ivory, bone, or wooden storyknives,
    the girls make drawings in mud or snow while
    relating the tale to other girls. Each village
    has a slightly different set of symbols though
    most all tellings are begun with a drawing of the
    basic setting. Tales told include child versions
    of adult folktales, myths, villages tales, and
    adaptations of movies or European tales. Part
    game and part verbal art, storyknifing has (had
    even more so in the past) a vital function, for
    its content expresses major beliefs, attitudes,
    and morals. Some of the storytellers are recog-
    nized as the best for the number of tales known,
    the quality of their voice, and their dramatic
    flair.

74. Armstrong, Helen. "Hero Tales for Telling." *Horn
    Book* 25:1 (January-February 1949): 9-15.

    Hero tales are meant to be told and have special
    appeal for children ten years and older.
    Armstrong lists hero tales suitable for telling
    "in story cycles" and gives helpful tips on editing
    the tales for telling.

75. Bailey, Carolyn Sherwin. *For the Story Teller:
     Story Telling and Stories to Tell*. Springfield,
     Mass.: Milton Bradley Company, 1913. Reprinted
     Detroit: Gale, 1971.

     One of the earliest American texts on storytelling,
     Bailey's work reflects our society's interest in
     the education and moral development of young chil-
     dren: "... we can almost mold character, and in-
     fluence a child's future life activity by means
     of the stories which we tell him." Bailey gives
     advice on selection (with emphasis on the appeal
     to the senses); preparation, including how to
     shorten a long story; presentation; and program
     planning. Stories should be "carefully prepared
     and presented happily." Stories stimulate emotions
     and thus stories that inspire fear should be
     avoided. Bailey also points out the value of
     storytelling in introducing children (both the
     foreign-born and the "average" American child) to
     "good" English. A model for storytellers for many
     years, Bailey's book has been superceded by more
     recent storytellings texts and is, today, primarily
     of historical interest.

76. Baker, Augusta, and Greene, Ellin. *Storytelling:
     Art and Technique*. New York: Bowker, 1977.

     Two distinguished librarian-storytellers share
     their insights on the creative and practical as-
     pects of storytelling. Written with economy
     and clarity, this handbook answers frequently
     asked questions on selection, preparation, pre-
     sentation, program planning, and administration
     of the library story hour program. The opening
     chapter presents a brief history of storytelling
     in American libraries. Includes a glossary and
     several useful bibliographies.

77. Barksdale, E.C., and Popp, Daniel. "The Teller with the Tale." *Fabula* 18 (1977): 249-255.

Each storytelling situation is a unique event, for each narrator's style is different and audiences are always changing. Different tellers and listeners will share a tale in different ways, suggesting that the future of folklore study lies in the study of the teller as well as of the tale. Examining three tellings of the same story, "The Vanishing Hitchhiker," the authors found many changes. One teller covered the saccharine with the miraculous, another matched cliche with brevity, and the third juxtaposed the real with the absurd. It is this very difference in telling style, perspective, and situation that is at the base of the distinction between mediocre tellers and the outstanding ones.

78. Bascom, William R. "Verbal Art." *Journal of American Folklore* 68:269 (July-September 1955): 245-252.

Bascom's early essay on the new term, "verbal art," provides an interesting background to the evolution of folklore study in general and how the study of storytelling has expanded. While still valuing the text of tales, researchers have come to realize that the folktale's medium is not just the work, but the spoken word and all it involves. Verbal art is intangible and forever changing; it endures only as long as it is repeated, having no true existence outside the minds of those who know it. This realization of the listener's role establishes the aesthetic experience of the audience as being simultaneous with the creative act. Verbal art "dies when people stop telling it, and when they learn it by reading, rather than by hearing it told by others."

79.   Basgoz, Ilhan. "The Tale-Singer and His Audience."
      In *Folklore: Performance and Communication,* edited
      by Dan Ben-Amos and Kenneth Goldstein. The Hague:
      Mouton, 1975.

      In each performance of a given story the teller and
      the telling are affected by the audience. The
      teller responds with his unique personality and
      background, and adds or deletes elements as a direct
      consequence of his ongoing interaction with the au-
      dience. The core narrative remains the same but
      length, details, interjections, and descriptions
      are altered in response to the audience's mood,
      setting, and educational background. Basgoz's
      teller was greatly affected by the difference in
      telling to peasants in a coffeehouse and to members
      of a teachers' union and the town elite in the Union
      Hall. His performance to the peasants was more
      warmly received, which led him to make it longer,
      funnier, and bawdier--the cycle of co-composing
      which occurs in all live story performances.

80.   Bauer, Caroline Feller. *Handbook for Storytellers.*
      Chicago: American Library Association, 1977.

      A former children's librarian, radio and television
      storyteller, and popular lecturer presents a grab
      bag of ideas, programs, techniques, and activities
      designed to liven up school and public library
      storyhours. Bauer places heavy emphasis on media,
      including film, music, crafts, and puppetry. She
      offers excellent suggestions for promoting story-
      telling, a subject bibliography, and sample pro-
      grams.

81.   Bauman, Richard. *Verbal Art as Performance.* Row-
      ley, Mass.: Newbury, 1977.

      Writing as a folklorist and linguistic anthropolo-
      gist, Bauman develops his view of storytelling as
      a verbal art performance in chapters dealing with

the nature, patterning, and quality of oral performance. This manner of study is an effort to balance
past tendencies where scholars studied the tale "at
the expense of its teller, telling and reception."
Bauman believes that focusing on performance may
open a new kind of folkloristics that is able to
comprehend a wider sense of human experience.
Bauman also includes a solid overview of various
philosophies dealing with storytelling and an outstanding bibliography of noted materials.

82.   Bone, Woutrina A. *Children's Stories and How to
       Tell Them*. New York: Harcourt, 1924. Reprinted
       Detroit: Gale, 1975.

       Bone was a lecturer in education at the University
       of Sheffield, England. Her remarks about fairylore
       and how much children should be exposed to fairylore
       (obviously a concern at the time of writing) are
       of interest and her chapter on "Picture Making and
       Word Choosing" covers this aspect of storytelling
       in greater depth than more recent storytelling
       texts. Primarily of historical interest.

83.   Breneman, Lucille N., and Breneman, Bren. *Once
       Upon a Time: A Storytelling Handbook*. Chicago:
       Nelson-Hall, 1983.

       Two teachers of drama and speech have written a
       handbook for "teachers, librarians, entertainers,
       speakers, and those in the helping professions,"
       who are caught up in the revival of the ancient art
       of storytelling. The emphasis is on storytelling
       as performance to an adult audience. There is a
       chapter on story biography in response to current
       interest in "roots." The annotated bibliography
       includes modern short stories and novels for inter-
       pretative reading as well as traditional literature.

84. Bryant, Sara Cone. *How to Tell Stories to Chil-
    dren*. Boston: Houghton Mifflin, 1905, 1924. Re-
    printed Detroit: Gale, 1973.

    Cited by Richard Alvey in his doctoral dissertation
    on organized storytelling as "the first lengthy
    and detailed American work devoted exclusively to
    the art of storytelling" Bryant's book helped to
    shape early organized storytelling to children in
    America. Bryant believed that a story is first of
    all a work of art and that the purpose of story-
    telling is to give joy. She offered teachers of
    kindergarten and primary grade children practical
    suggestions for selecting and adapting stories to
    tell to children of different ages, techniques of
    telling, and "secondary" storytelling activities,
    such as having children retell the story or draw
    pictures inspired by the story. Her book includes
    the texts of thirty-two stories adapted for telling
    and arranged according to grade levels.

85. Chambers, Aidan. "Storytelling and Reading Aloud."
    In *Introducing Books to Children*. Second edition,
    completely revised and expanded. Boston: Horn Book,
    1983, pp. 129-156.

    A practical guide for introducing literature to
    children through the arts of storytelling and read-
    ing aloud. Chambers' article on children as story-
    tellers, "Letter from England: Having Fun Being
    Famous," originally published in the *Horn Book* mag-
    azine, is included in full.

86. Colwell, Eileen. *Storytelling*. London: Bodley
    Head, 1980.

    This practical and reassuring guide for librarians,
    teachers, playgroup leaders, parents, and other
    would-be storytellers is based on the author's forty
    plus years' experience as a storyteller and former
    children's librarian in England. Colwell is com-

parable to the esteemed American storyteller,
Augusta Baker, both in her joy of sharing literature
with children and in her mastery of the storyteller's art. In contrast to Baker, Colwell often
adapts stories for telling and her book includes a
chapter on this aspect of telling as well as chapters on selection, preparation, and presentation.

87. Cosentino, Donald. *Defiant Maids and Stubborn
Farmers: Tradition and Invention in Mende Story
Performance*. Cambridge: Cambridge University Press,
1982.

With an "appreciation of the web which binds tale
to teller, teller to audience, and the ensemble to
its society," Cosentino examines the different forms
of storytelling in Mende society. While everyone
performs tales to some degree, only a few become
the equivalent of professional storytellers, travel-
ing about the country and living off their performances alone. It is these professionals that employ
song, dance, and costume to enhance their performances that not only assist the story, but in some
cases dominate the performance. Settings are most
often semi-formal, on lit verandahs in the evening.
Mende audiences above all want to be entertained,
causing one storyteller to observe: "Nowadays, ordinary people like the stories for the music and
the entertainment; they don't know the stories have
sense."

88. Crabbe, Katharyn. "Folk over Fakelore: But Is It
Art?" *School Library Journal* 26:3 (November 1979):
42-43.

"As artists, tellers of folktales must be capable
of re-creating each story so that it seems to have
grown naturally." This does not necessarily mean
a literal translation, for good folklore does not
automatically make good literature. The reteller's
goal is to give the impression that his language

is the original one of that tale, to give a sense
of the style of the original language, but not be
chained to its literal syntax and form. Retellers
must be true to the world of the original, but must
also work to make that world of story live for new
audiences.

89. Crowley, Daniel J. *I Could Talk Old-Story Good:
     Creativity in Bahamian Folklore.* Folklore Studies
     #17. Berkeley: University of California Press,
     1966.

     As the study of storytelling and folklore matured,
     the predominant theories concerning the teller's
     role evolved from one of human echo in which change
     in the text of any kind was deplored as being syn-
     onymous with decay to one of a broader and more
     anthropological base in which the storyteller is
     allowed the more creative imagination of a novelist
     and in which the tale is seen as a continually
     evolving art form. Crowley finds "that to be a
     traditional Bahamian storyteller, one is required
     to create. Without at least a little creative ef-
     fort, no story can come into being" and that the
     choosing, arranging, and performing of a story are
     major factors and contributions of each storyteller.

90. De Wit, Dorothy. *Children's Faces Looking Up: Pro-
     gram Building for the Storyteller.* Chicago: Ameri-
     can Library Association, 1979.

     A former children's services librarian draws upon
     almost twenty years' experience to inform beginning
     storytellers about the elements of good programming.
     Includes six demonstration programs and an extensive
     bibliography of sources of program material.

91. Farnsworth, Kathryn. "Storytelling in the Classroom
    --Not an Impossible Dream." *Language Arts* 58:2
    (February 1981): 162-167.

    Stressing the idea that telling stories is a process
    that improves with experience, Farnsworth offers
    suggestions for learning stories and exercises to
    enhance one's telling that can be used by both adult
    and child. Allowing students to begin telling
    shorter stories to younger children in settings
    free of competition helps them begin to enjoy tell-
    ing stories to their peers as well. And as story-
    telling develops within their peer groups it becomes
    an ongoing experience in the curriculum that fosters
    not only literature and language, but listening as
    well.

92. Glassie, Henry. *Passing the Time in Ballymenone:
    Culture and History of an Ulster Community.* Phila-
    delphia: University of Pennsylvania Press, 1982.

    Glassie's massive folklore study of an Irish com-
    munity ranges from festivals to homes and furniture.
    Of excellent quality and interest to storytellers
    is the chapter "Silence, Speech, Story, Song" that
    explores local storytelling from the inside out.
    Area tellers not only offer stories, but philoso-
    phies and criteria for good tellings, though they
    find it difficult to speak of stories apart from
    their specific tellers. Lamenting that some only
    "tell from the teeth out," local tellers emphasize
    the personal connection with stories told and the
    personal touch regarding words and description.
    Words can ornament tales, but more "important in
    the decoration of a story are key words, deep in
    meaning, repeated precisely and peppered through
    the text, appearing in its prosy and poetic sections
    to unify the whole." Regarded as a skill of indi-
    viduals regardless of educational background,
    Glassie's informants believe storytelling to be a
    double gift of words and vision, and of knowing
    how to combine the two.

93. Grider, Sylvia. "From the Tale to the Telling:
     AT366." In *Folklore on Two Continents,* edited by
     Nikolai Burlakoff. Bloomington: Indiana University
     Press, 1980, pp. 49-55.

     Realizing that many folktales change their genre
     or form from place to place or over time, Grider
     examines the tale best known in the U.S. as "The
     Golden Arm" and its various tellings. At times a
     "jump tale," at others a ghost tale, and still oth-
     ers a legend, the study of this one tale made Grider
     conclude that "the way it is told to and perceived
     by the audience determines the narrative category
     to which it belongs." Of value as well is the au-
     thor's discussion of how the "jump tale" works when
     the story literally reaches out and yanks the audi-
     ence. "For a split second, the fantasy becomes
     reality. The screaming and grabbing of the narrator
     unleashes a horrific epiphany as the audience shares
     the punishment of the fictional thief."

94. Handoo, Jawaharlal. "Style in Oral Narrative."
     In *Current Trends in Folklore*. India: University
     of Mysore, Institute of Kannada Studies, 1978, pp.
     16-30.

     As the folktale does not truly exist except when
     being told and shared between teller and listeners,
     the context and style of the teller are vital to
     the story's evaluation and study. Structure is
     basic, but language is only a part of an oral nar-
     rative for sound and gesture are also strong ele-
     ments in the sharing of tales between teller and
     audience. It is therefore important in the rela-
     tionship of tale, teller, and listener that the
     teller take an emotional stance toward the story
     and be faithful to himself, for the tale will break
     down if there is dishonesty or disbelief in the
     performance.

95. Hoppal, Mihaly. "Folk Narrative and Memory Processes." In *Folklore on Two Continents,* edited by Nikolai Burlakoff. Bloomington: Indiana University Press, 1980, pp. 281-289.

Memory, the essential element in oral narratives, should be the focus of both text and context studies of folktales. Though memory has been slow to become a source of study, numerous theories and levels are now being explored. Offering an overview, Hoppal discusses the basic shape of narrative memory by which general outlines are usually constant while details are frequently altered. Both short- and long-term memory come into play with regard to folk narratives, each affecting the other. "Recall in folk narratives is not mere reproduction, rather it involves reasoning and explanations ... [memory] is based on rationalization of various sorts, and on current knowledge of the person." One's beliefs and knowledge directly determine the words one uses to tell a given tale. While it is invisible and therefore difficult to study, Hoppal feels memory must be examined in regard to folktales and that an interdisciplinary approach would be most productive.

96. Iarusso, Marilyn Berg. "Storytelling: Revival of An Age-Old Art." *American Educator* 9:4 (Winter 1985): 36-40.

Drawing on her experience as Storytelling Specialist at the New York Public Library and guest storyteller at many schools, Iarusso suggests ways of incorporating storytelling into the curriculum through language arts, reading, writing, social studies, oral speaking, and research skills. She reiterates the values of storytelling in the classroom--rapport between teachers and children, appreciation of literature and drama, motivation to read, a help in organizing thinking skills, introduction to world cultures, etc. Iarusso offers helpful tips for finding, learning, and presenting stories to children. She encourages teachers who are anxious about "telling" to begin by reading aloud to their students. A section set off from the main text highlights successful school programs, including the annual storytelling contest sponsored by the New York City Board of Education, a program at the Brearly School in New York City in which sixth-grade students tell stories to younger children, and an after-school storytelling club at Eagle Hill Middle School in a suburb of Syracuse, N.Y.

97. Johnson, Terry D. "Presenting Literature to Children." *Children's Literature in Education* 10:1 (Spring 1979): 35-43.

Johnson believes adults "are crucial to the child's joyful and productive entry into the world of literature." He describes activities that make literary sense, such as asking children to predict what is going to happen next in the story, and warns against advanced vocabulary preparation and unrelated arts and crafts activities--the "pin-the-tail-on-Eeyore" school. Activities should send the reader/listener back to the story, either via memory or by rereading.

98. Labrie, Vivian. "How Can We Understand the Retention of a Folktale?" In *Folklore on Two Continents,* edited by Nikolai Burlakoff. Bloomington: Indiana University Press, 1980, pp. 286-299.

Aware that there are two levels of retention in regard to folktales (teller to teller and within each teller), Labrie primarily examines the role of memory within the teller. Viewing memory as a reconstructive process, Labrie sees the retelling of tales as involving elements gathered during the time since the tale was last told or heard, thus explaining in part the continual evolution of folktales in general. "The knowledge of the tale can be seen as a bank of memorized kernels of informa-

tion--concepts, expressions, motifs--which consti-
tute the narrative universe" and each narration
then becomes an individual blend of memory, creativity, and stylistic ability. Labrie includes
references to the variety of research being done
on memory and urges folklorists to draw from all
related sources as a way of enhancing their own
understanding of this process that is the core of
folklore.

99. Larrick, Nancy. "Poetry in the Story Hour." *Top
of the News* 32:2 (January 1976): 151-161.

A gifted educator and poetry anthologist suggests
ways of involving children in poetry: impromptu
choral reading, use of background music for the
reading of a poem, body movement and interpretive
dance, and impromptu dramatization or pantomime.
Her enthusiastic response to "poetry happenings"
in workshops and classroom situations will inspire
the novice to attempt similar programs.

100. Martin, Sue Ann. "Techniques for the Creative
Reading or Telling of Stories to Children." *Elementary English* 45:5 (May 1968): 611-618.

Martin believes it is "imperative to give storytelling prime time in the social and psychological
diet of children" and discusses various elements
involved in sharing tales well. Imagery being
especially important, Martin divides it into tac-
tile, olfactory, auditory, kinesthetic, and visual,
and explores how each is vital to a good telling
and aids in involving the listener. The vocal
pause and timing are solidly though briefly covered, as is the use of gestures which Martin feels
are best when spontaneous and rise from the teller's involvement with the story. A basic bibliography of materials on storytelling is included.

101.   Mathy, Margaret. "Folklore and Flapjacks." *Top
        of the News* 28:2 (January 1972): 198-201.

        "Folklore and Flapjacks" is a family-style story
        program sponsored by the Children's Department of
        the Dayton and Montgomery County (Ohio) Public
        Library and broadcast on radio Sunday mornings.
        The author, a branch librarian and the radio story-
        teller, presents tips on selecting and presenting
        stories on radio. Includes sample programs.

102.   Middleswarth, Victoria. "Folklore Books for Chil-
        dren: Guidelines for Selection." *Top of the News*
        34:4 (Summer 1978): 348-352.

        As an academic discipline folklore deserves the
        same scholarship and careful evaluation as materi-
        als on English or history. Middleswarth outlines
        major points of consideration in evaluating all
        books on folklore and especially those for chil-
        dren, believing scholarship should extend to all
        age levels. Good editions and adaptations of folk
        narratives should preserve the ethnic flavor of
        the originals and provide some form of documenta-
        tion ranging in depth from academic source notes
        to a prose introduction of the tale's background.
        Inclusion of contextual information--the place and
        manner in which the tales were originally told--
        is also a vital addition to any children's folklore
        book and can add much to one's appreciation of the
        stories and culture.

103.   Nesbitt, Elizabeth. "The Art of Storytelling."
        Horn Book 21:6 (November-December 1945): 439-444.

        Storytelling, rightly practiced, is a strong edu-
        cational force. "It (storytelling) has dealt with,
        helped to preserve, and interpreted anew for each
        generation the accumulated wisdom of the literature
        of all ages and all peoples.... It is one method
        whereby the hearts and minds of children may be

opened to the fact that the present stems from
the past, that we of the new world share a common
heritage with those of the old." In closing,
Nesbitt notes the work of the Radio Broadcast and
Recording Committee of the Division of Libraries
for Children and Young People of the American Library Association to make available "in the form
of records, stories told by some of the great
storytellers of the present day," and describes
the first such records made by Gudrun Thorne-
Thomsen.

104. New York Library Association. Children's and Young
People's Section. *Once Upon a Time*. Revised edition. New York: New York Public Library, 1964.

A concise pamphlet that discusses the philosophy
of the library preschool hour, picture-book hour,
and story hour for older children, and suggests
materials and techniques for successful storytelling programs. Sample programs and a bibliography
for each age group are included. Prepared by a
committee of seven library storytellers, chaired
by Augusta Baker, then Storytelling Specialist at
the New York Public Library.

105. Noss, Philip A. "The Performance of the Gbaya
Tale." In *Forms of Folklore in Africa: Narrative,
Poetic, Gnomic, Dramatic*. Edited by Bernth
Lindfors. Austin: University of Texas Press, 1977,
pp. 135-143.

Believing that "in the tale are found the words
of the ancestors; in the performer is found the
link between the past and the present" all Gbaya
peoples share stories. The most skilled teller
uses four primary devices as he works with the
audience to create an entertaining and meaningful
performance: (1) Personalization--involves local
descriptions, people, and at times the teller himself becomes a character in the story, (2) Song--

invites active and physical participation that
draws in the listener, but that must also be con-
trolled so that no one steals the stage from the
story; (3) Ideophones--the use of onomonopoetic
sounds that add to the action and sensory description of the story; (4) Conclusion--the teller's
individual explanation (not rewriting) of the story's end that still leaves the deepest meanings
to be found within the story's characters and their
relationships.

106.   Olajubu, Chief Oludare.   "Yoruba Verbal Artists
and Their Work."   *Journal of American Folklore* 91:
360 (April-June 1978): 675-690.

Yoruba verbal artists must possess a good memory,
a sweet voice, quick wit, a sense of humor, and a
deep interest in their art as well.   The many forms
or genres of verbal art are divided by the occupa-
tion or religion into which one is born, and only
the entitled can share those songs or stories.
But regardless of the genre, most tellers learn
from childhood by imitation at public performances.
One important distinction in Yoruba verbal art is
the difference between the chants and histories
that must be memorized, the tellers of which are
greatly valued, and the folktales that are seen
as common property, the tellers of which receive
admiration, but no financial reward.   Performance
is the essence of Yoruba telling and the "audience
is perhaps the most important influence on the performance ... every performance is for and about
the audience, and the main objectives of the artist
are to entertain, amuse, and impress the audience
so as to earn praise, admiration, and material
gifts."

107. Partridge, Emelyn, and Partridge, George. *Story-telling in School and Home*. New York: Sturgis and Walton, 1912.

   The Partridges provide a rich exploration of story-telling's relationship to children from a variety of perspectives, ranging from religion to school, groups to individuals, and fables to epics. Basic "how to" chapters are balanced with psychological explorations of the interaction of teller and child and story which conclude that the child responds in deeply personal ways far beyond simple pleasure. "In every mood, feeling, sentiment he is carrying on a busy world building" and from this comes "the connected ideals and valuations of his whole life; and those permanent moods and sentiments which are the foundation of character and give to life its deepest meaning."

108. Peek, Philip M. "The Power of Words in African Verbal Arts." *Journal of American Folklore* 94:371 (January-March 1981): 19-43.

   In this survey of African cultures and verbal art Peek examines the important value placed on the spoken word and its near tangible sense of reality. These peoples who feel the ability to speak well is a primary social concern are naturally and es-pecially aware of their storytelling. Tellers are highly regarded as vessels of speech and his-tory, and function as memory and symbol with their verbal creations being primarily symbolic rather than literal, but always "true." In many situa-tions the teller is seen not just as the presenter, but the actualizer of the narrative so that others may feel and see it. As he tells it he becomes the story and as the tale lives on through his retellings he lives on through the story he tells. The importance and value placed on verbal art cause Peek to conclude that it is the verbal component far more than the time and setting that defines a storytelling event. "Art pervades life--it does not just decorate," and storytelling is one of those arts.

109.   Pellowski, Anne. *The World of Storytelling.* New York: Bowker, 1977.

A comprehensive and scholarly work, *The World of Storytelling* is a primary source for all interested in folktales and storytelling. Pellowski discusses the chronological history of storytelling from ancient bard to library teller, and religious, theatrical, and institutional tellings around the world. By examining storytelling styles and situations in numerous cultures Pellowski not only provides information, but also opens up storytelling to its fullest potential for contemporary tellers. And as tellers in all times and cultures had to somehow learn their art, the book closes with an overview of training methods from inherited position to inservice workshop sessions. Of additional value is Pellowski's outstanding bibliography of related books and periodicals.

110.   Pittsburgh. Carnegie Library. *Story Hour Courses.* Pittsburgh, 1902-.

The Carnegie Library of Pittsburgh was known for its story hour cycles centered around great literature (see Olcott, item 14). Courses listing stories to be told, sources to consult, and how to prepare and tell the story were prepared for the storytellers. Among the courses published were *King Arthur and the Knights of the Round Table* (1902), *Story Telling to Children from Norse Mythology and the Nibelungenlied* (1903), *Story Hour Courses for Children from Greek Myths, the Iliad and the Odyssey* (1903), *Stories from the Norse* (1914), and *Stories of Rustum* (1928-29).

111.   Rooth, Anna Birgitta. *The Importance of Story-
        telling: A Study Based on Field Work in Northern
        Alaska.* Studia Ethnologica Upsaliensia Vol. 1.
        Stockholm: Almqvist & Wiksell International, 1976.

        Rooth's respect for her informants and their sto-
        ries is very evident in this report of storytelling
        among the Eskimos in Alaska and Greenland. Her
        study covered the proper times for storytelling,
        oral styles of narration, rules and taboos con-
        nected with storytelling, and the functions of the
        storyteller in Eskimo culture. Rooth cautions the
        Western reader against applying inappropriate cri-
        teria in judging Eskimo storytelling and emphasizes
        the importance of storytelling in enculturation.
        The report is slim in size, rich in content.

112.   Ross, Eulalie Steinmetz. "To Tell a Story." In
        The Lost Half-Hour. New York: Harcourt, 1963,
        pp. 181-191.

        A former supervisor of storytelling at the New
        York Public Library offers the neophyte practical
        advice on selecting and learning a story, preparing
        children to listen, and telling the story. The
        storyteller is "only an instrument through which
        the story flows...." The most important ingredient
        in good telling is sincerity. This essay appeared
        in slightly different form in *Horn Book* 39 (1963):
        253-258.

113.   Ross, Ramon Royal. *Storyteller.* Second edition.
        Columbus: Merrill, 1972.

        As our culture develops a renewed interest in
        people-to-people activities, storytelling grows
        in variety and popularity. Employing our natural
        need for being with people, storytelling, believes
        Ross, has much to offer everyone, for it is the
        magic that happens during the sharing that is the
        most vital aspect of telling. Still, quality and

style are important and Ross examines elements of
finding, learning, and telling stories with sample
tales and practice activities at the end of each
chapter. Chapters on gathering tales and telling
personal experience stories reflect various elements of the oral tradition and the teller's personal connection with what he tells. The strength
of a story lies in the fascination it holds for
the teller and it is that fascination that is
transmitted to the listeners and creates the magic
that makes it all worthwhile.

114.   Sawyer, Ruth. "A Storyteller's Approach to Chil-
       dren's Books." In *The Contents of the Basket:
       And Other Papers on Children's Books and Reading,*
       edited by Frances Lander Spain. New York: New
       York Public Library, 1960, pp. 51-59.

       Sawyer recommends taking time in the story hour
       to introduce children to books--new titles and
       older titles in danger of being forgotten. She
       cites specific titles she has used successfully,
       including *Daniel Boone,* by James Daugherty, *Amos
       Fortune, Free Man,* by Elizabeth Yates, and *The
       Wind in the Willows,* by Kenneth Grahame. This
       article was originally presented as an Anne Carroll
       Moore lecture at the New York Public Library.

115.   Sawyer, Ruth. *The Way of the Storyteller.* New
       York: Viking, 1942.

       Sawyer thoughtfully discusses all elements of
       storytelling from its place as an ancient and liv-
       ing folk art through one's own building of back-
       ground and style to the art of selecting the right
       tale for the right time. Her information is sound
       and encouraging and far more than simply a "how to"
       text. Few writers or tellers could better support
       via their own lives her statements that one must
       have a clear understanding of what storytelling
       is and is not, and, that the art of telling "lies

within the storyteller, to be searched for, drawn
out, made to grow." Demonstrating her belief that
to be a good storyteller one must be "gloriously
alive," Sawyer discusses her own joys and troubles
with storytelling from childhood through her days
as one of America's leading storytellers. Con-
cluding the book are eleven of Sawyer's favorite
tales, bibliographies of further materials for
telling aloud to children, and books for background
reading for the teller.

116.   Sayers, Frances Clarke. "The Storyteller's Art."
In *Summoned by Books*. New York: Viking, 1965,
pp. 99-106.

Through storytelling the child is introduced to
great literature and the elements of creative art
--"originality, style, structure and form, charac-
terization, mood and atmosphere, and the beauty
of words." Folklore is an inexhaustible source
for the storyteller and trains one in judging the
telling quality in modern stories. The secret of
telling well lies in the art of *seeing*. This essay, under the title "Enriching Literature Through
Storytelling," was first published in 1953 by the
Association for Childhood Education International
as part of their series, *Adventuring in Literature
with Children*.

117.   Sayers, Frances Clarke. "Storytelling." In *Anthology of Children's Literature,* by Edna Johnson,
et al. Boston: Houghton Mifflin, 1970, Appendix
A, pp. 1141-1147.

A distinguished librarian-storyteller distills
the principles of storytelling. "The one immutable
law of storytelling is to see with your inner eye
everything of which you speak." In addition to
this piece the introductions to each genre in the
anthology provide helpful background for new storytellers.

118. Scheub, Harold.   "Body and Image in Oral Narrative
      Performance." *New Literary History* 8:3 (Spring
      1977): 345-367.

      Not only does the body establish a physical rela-
      tionship between artist and audience during an
      oral performance, it also functions as an artistic
      medium that expands the text and bridges the phys-
      ical and social aspects. "In a performance members
      of the audience are immersed in images" both in-
      ternal and external. Gestures may demonstrate
      something in the story, count, emphasize, create
      an illusion of time passed, create punctuation,
      add to the characterization, and even replace
      words, especially ideophones. The movements of
      the artist's body both in direct conjunction with
      the tale's images and words and on its own aid
      the creation of shared images. Just as the sounds
      and verbal rhythms used reflect the narrative pat-
      terns, so do the teller's movements and expres-
      sions.

119. Scheub, Harold.   "Oral Narrative Process and the
      Use of Models." *New Literary History* 6:2 (Winter
      1975): 353-377.

      With image being the core of oral narratives, the
      sharing of a tale is dependent on a base of shared
      experiences that can foster images. The artist
      evokes an image with words and the audience re-
      sponds by creating its own. Scheub finds the tools
      needed for this process to be developed at an early
      age in South African societies due to the chil-
      dren's ongoing exposure to stories, the repetition
      of stories, and the repetition of phrases and im-
      ages within stories. As their thematic and imagery
      backgrounds increase so does their emotional re-
      lationship to the story. It is in this way--
      through shared images and emotions--that the sto-
      ry's message is transmitted. "Whatever the mes-
      sage, the *performance* is the thing, the experience
      of the image is the thing" because the audience
      is involved with the creating of images.

120.   Schimmel, Nancy. *Just Enough to Make a Story: A
       Sourcebook for Storytelling*. Berkeley, Calif.:
       Sisters' Choice Press, 1978. Second edition, 1982.

       Storyteller Nancy Schimmel is known for her relaxed
       style, feminist attitude, and use of paperfolding,
       fingerplays, and music to enhance the telling.
       Her book is a reflection of herself and offers a
       rich mix. It includes visual stories, stories
       with songs, and an annotated index to "active her-
       oines in folktales for children."

121.   Scott, Edna (Lyman). *Storytelling: What to Tell
       and How to Tell It*. Chicago: McClurg & Co., 1911.
       Reprinted Detroit: Singing Tree Press, 1971.

       This early handbook on storytelling is addressed
       to "mothers, teachers, and librarians" who are
       interested in the use of storytelling "as a phase
       of another occupation." Recognizing the need for
       proper preparation, Lyman advocates reading aloud
       if the nonprofessional does not have sufficient
       time for learning to tell. She offers advice on
       the selection of stories, includes the complete
       text of fourteen tales recommended for children,
       and discusses the values of biography and epic
       tales and the importance of program planning.
       Scott, formerly children's librarian in Oak Park,
       Illinois, was one of the first library storytellers
       to leave her position to become a professional
       storyteller and a lecturer on children's literature
       and storytelling. Her text is primarily of histor-
       ical interest.

122.   Seitel, Peter. *See So That We May See: Perform-
       ances and Interpretations of Traditional Tales
       From Tanzania*. Bloomington: Indiana University
       Press, 1980.

       Drawing from personal field work, Seitel shares
       and examines the storytelling process among the

Haya of Tanzania. The book's title, which is a
traditional beginning to a storytelling session,
reflects Seitel's concern for the interaction of
storyteller and listener as well as the text. At-
tempting to share style and emotion as well as
words, the thirty-five stories have been tran-
scribed in a fascinating and different manner.
Space between words, letters, and sentences is
used to represent silence. Size of typeface indicates volume and tone, and line breaks show pacing. Through discussion and stories Seitel draws
the reader in as he feels the storyteller must.
"The two sides of storytelling, the significance
of events as they are perceived and communicated
by a narrator, and the spontaneous, aesthetic experience of the performance itself, reinforce one
another through a narrator's ability to interpret
and enact imagined events from different points
of view. Rich performances proceed from rich interpretations."

123.   Shedlock, Marie. *The Art of the Story-Teller*.
       Originally published by D. Appleton & Company,
       1915. Reprinted New York: Dover, 1951.

       More than any other person Marie Shedlock influ-
       enced the development of storytelling in American
       libraries and classrooms. Shedlock considered
       storytelling "mini-drama" and the child's natural
       introduction to literature. In addition to guide-
       lines for telling, the book includes eighteen sto-
       ries chosen by Ms. Shedlock and an annotated bib-
       liography of 135 additional story titles compiled
       for the revised edition by Eulalie Steinmetz, who
       was Supervisor of Storytelling at the New York
       Public Library.

124. Smith, Lillian. "The Art of the Fairy Tale." In
The Unreluctant Years. Chicago: American Library
Association, 1953, pp. 44-63.

The former head of Boys and Girls House in Toronto
discusses the role that fairy tales play in the
child's literary and imaginative development. The
form and language of the folktale give aesthetic
pleasure to the child, satisfy the imagination,
and reflect the culture and environment of the
people from whom they come. The beauty of fairy
tales lies "not only in their deeper meaning but
also in their manner of telling, the music and
rhythm of words." The author uses the full text
of "The Sleeping Beauty" and "The Three Billy Goats
Gruff" and excerpts from several other traditional
tales to demonstrate her points.

125. Steinmetz, Eulalie. "Storytelling Versus Recordings." *Horn Book* 24:3 (May-June 1948): 163-172.

A former supervisor of storytelling at the New
York Public Library expresses her concerns about
the use of story recordings in the story hour.
"Storytelling is a twofold relationship made up
of teller and listener.... To sacrifice the play
of personality upon personality, the creation of
mood, the influence for good, is to sacrifice those
attributes which make up the living heart of storytelling." Steinmentz is critical of the storytelling talents of the narrators--"There is nothing
of interpretative skill, of creative artistry, of
imaginative release." She makes one exception:
the recordings of Gudrun Thorne-Thomsen. Steinmetz
encourages the use of recordings of gifted tellers
with students of storytelling. The article presents excellent criteria for evaluating recordings
for children and serves as an antidote to those
who would substitute "the mechanical for the human"
in contemporary society.

126. Stone, Kay, and Davis, Donald. "To Ease the Heart:
      Traditional Storytelling." *National Storytelling
      Journal* 1:1 (Winter 1984): 3-6.

      Interweaving essay by Stone and conversational
      monologue by Davis, these storytellers examine
      and reflect on the differences between traditional
      storytelling and more contemporary telling in per-
      formance. Traditional tellers who grew up living
      with stories tell them informally, letting the
      story put the facial expressions and particular
      words and body movement into the teller. In con-
      trast, the story performer prepares for large au-
      diences in a theatrical way and often works to
      overwhelm with a highly studied performance. The
      telling and performing of stories will always dif-
      fer, but both can work toward the vital balance
      between creator and creation which allows the
      teller and tale to meet and connect.

127. Storytelling Issue. *Horn Book* 59:3 (June 1983):
      242-384.

      In response to renewed interest *Horn Book*--for the
      first time since 1934--devoted an entire issue to
      the art of storytelling. Contents: "What Is Story-
      telling?" by Eileen Colwell; "A Peculiar Under-
      standing: Re-Creating the Literary Fairy Tale,"
      by Ellin Greene; "Storytelling," by Jackie
      Torrence; "'Words in Our Hearts': The Experience
      of the Story," by Laura Simms; "On Story and Story-
      telling: A Conversation," by Diane Wolkstein and
      James Wiggins; and "Storytelling New and Old," by
      Padraic Colum.

128. Stotter, Ruth. "The Storyteller: Bridge Between
      Cultures." *The National Storytelling Journal* 2:4
      (Fall 1985): 20-23.

      Stotter discusses the problems for the non-Indian
      who attempts to tell native American stories. The

storyteller must know something about the culture
from which the story comes, the story's significance for the people who created it, and the world-
view it reflects. "Storytellers adapting texts
from other cultures have an inherent responsibility
to both the culture from which they derived the
story and to their audiences. It is important
that the central ideas of the tale not be altered."

129. Swanson, Barbara. "Participation Storytelling."
      School Library Journal 31:8 (April 1985): 48.

Involving children in the telling—-joining in a
refrain or acting out the story with the librarian
as narrator--is rewarding for both teller and listeners. Swanson, Children's Coordinator at Kern
County Library System in Bakersfield, California,
describes her approach and names some of the titles
she has used successfully with preschoolers and
elementary school children. Fun for everyone,
this type of storytelling works especially well
with children whose use of English is limited and
with reluctant or non-readers.

130. Taylor, Mary Agnes. "The Folk Tale: Literature
      for All Ages?" *School Library Journal* 20:7 (March
      1974): 80-81.

The author questions the designation "for all ages"
assigned to folk tales. "The simple story line
which satisfied early readers is not sufficiently
engaging to hold the interest of average middle-
range readers. However, these children have not
yet attained the degree of sophistication necessary
to read stories for their complex symbolic meaning.
Middle graders are at once too old and not old
enough to appreciate the folk tale." Taylor makes
some valid points, but her argument is weakened
by her limited knowledge of folk tales that appeal
to the middle group. Her article serves to remind
storytellers of the importance of wise selection.

131. Thorne-Thomsen, Gudrun. *Storytelling and Stories
      I Tell*. New York: Viking, 1956.

      This pamphlet, published in memory of the gifted
      Norwegian storyteller, includes her versions of
      "The Pancake" and "Peter, Paul and Espen Cinder
      Lad" with comments about their appeal to children.
      Thorne-Thomsen relates her experiences telling to
      children, ages six to fifteen, in the libraries
      of the park houses in Chicago. She writes about
      the values of storytelling and describes her ap-
      proach to learning a story. Unlike her contempo-
      raries Marie Shedlock and Sara Cone Bryant, Thorne-
      Thomsen never wrote a textbook on storytelling.
      Storytellers treasure this piece made public by
      her son Francis.

132. Tooze, Ruth. *Storytelling*. Englewood Cliffs,
      N.J.: Prentice-Hall, 1959.

      At the time of publication this was one of the
      outstanding books on storytelling and is still
      helpful today. The author, then Director of the
      Children's Caravan, wrote to inspire teachers and
      others to tell stories "as a means of sharing,
      teaching, and entertaining." Tooze believed that
      anyone could be a storyteller. She emphasized
      the importance of building on one's personal qual-
      ities and experience and the value of reading
      "good and great literature" in the process of be-
      coming a storyteller. In addition to discussions
      of selection, preparation, and presentation, the
      book includes twenty stories, a story poem, and
      three ballads as well as an extensive bibliography
      of background reading.

133. Ziskind, Sylvia. *Telling Stories to Children*.
      New York: Wilson, 1976.

      A straightforward text on storytelling, covering
      selection, preparation, and telling, program plan-

ning, poetry in the story hour, and creative dramatics. The author, a former librarian who also holds a master's degree in speech arts, offers tips on the use of the voice and exercises to relieve tension. The extensive bibliography includes books on voice and speech, creative dramatics, story and poetry collections, foreign-language books to use with their English counterparts, etc.

IV. STORYTELLING IN SPECIAL SETTINGS OR
     TO GROUPS WITH SPECIAL NEEDS

Story is very close to liturgy, which is why
one's children like to have the story repeated
exactly as they heard it the night before.

> Hugh Hood
> "The Short Story"
> *The Kenyon Review*

A. Young Children

134.   Baar-Lindsay, Christopher.   "Library Programming
       for Toddlers."   *Public Libraries* 22:3 (Fall 1983):
       111-113.

       The children's librarian for the Henderson County
       (N.C.) Public Library offers inexperienced tellers
       to children under age three concrete guidelines
       for program planning and evaluation based on her
       own successful program.   The article includes a
       sample program and an evaluation form for parents
       to complete.   The form provides patron input and
       program justification.

135.   Caples, Beth.   *Story Hour for the Three to Five
       Year Old*.   Revised edition.   Baltimore, Md.: Enoch
       Pratt Free Library, 1958.

       Enoch Pratt was a leader in story hours for pre-
       schoolers.   This attractive pamphlet covers the
       characteristics of three to five year olds, what
       they like in their books, and how to plan and con-
       duct a successful preschool story hour program.
       Includes a list of suitable books to share with
       young children and sources of finger plays and
       singing games.

136.   Foster, Joanna. *How to Conduct Effective Picture Book Programs: A Handbook*. New York: Westchester Library System, 1967.

Written to accompany the film, "The Pleasure is Mutual: How to Conduct Effective Picture Book Programs," this handbook reinforces the principles illustrated in the film and lists picture books to use with pre-school age children.

137.   Greene, Ellin. "Pre-School Story Hour Today." *Top of the News* 31:1 (November 1974): 80-85.

This follow-up to an article written by the author in 1961 (see item 141) indicates the growing acceptance of the preschool story hour as a regular part of library service to children and the use of multimedia (films, filmstrips, recordings, and toys) in preschool programs. Greene gives suggestions for making preschool hours effective and pleasurable. (Note that "preschool" here refers to three- to five-year-olds, as Toddler Hours for the eighteen-month- to three-year-olds were just beginning.)

138.   Horner, Margaret L. "Pre-School Storytelling: A Reappraisal." *Wilson Library Bulletin* 37:4 (December 1962): 335-337.

Gary Public Library, Indiana, began its Preschool Storytime in 1945. Seventeen years later the staff reevaluated the program to determine if it was worth the time and effort required. Such things as publicity, organization, and presentation were examined through a review of past practices and a workshop was held to improve performance. The storytellers decided to emphasize books and to subordinate flannelgraphs, recordings, finger plays, and activity games to distinguish the library's program from programs offered at nursery schools and other community agencies. Attendance at the story times and book circulation increased as a result.

139. Kewish, Nancy. "South Euclid's Pilot Project for Two-Year-Olds and Parents." *School Library Journal* 25:7 (March 1979): 93-98.

This report of a six-week pilot project held in the fall of 1977 gives practical advice for developing a library program for toddlers and their parents. It covers the characteristics of two-year-olds as they relate to program planning; suitable materials--stories, recordings, and filmstrips; publicity; registration; an orientation meeting for the parents; and the program itself. The article includes a copy of the parents' evaluation form and a list of recommended books for two-year-olds and for parents of two-year-olds.

140. Moore, Vardine. *Pre-School Story Hour*. Second edition. Metuchen, N.J.: Scarecrow, 1972.

A useful handbook for librarians and others who plan and conduct story hours for three-to-five-year-olds. The author presents library practices and procedures, values of the preschool story hour, characteristics of young children, program planning for preschoolers (with sample programs), suggested concurrent programs for parents, and the use of music, pantomime, puppetry, films, and other activities in the preschool story hour. Includes a list of books that appeal to young children.

141. Peterson, Ellin F. "Pre-School Hour." *Top of the News* 18 (December 1961): 47-51.

The development of the library storytelling program for three-to-five-year-olds, its purpose and values. For many children the preschool hour is an introduction to literature and art and the child's first opportunity to select books for home reading. Peterson outlines the requirements for a successful preschool hour and describes a sample program.

142.   Shaw, Spencer G. "First Steps: Storytime with Young Listeners." In *Start Early for an Early Start: You and the Young Child,* edited by Ferne Johnson. Chicago: American Library Association, 1976, pp. 41-64.

Shaw presents detailed guidelines for a successful preschool storytelling program, covering objectives, planning, and scheduling, publicity, program content, the use of book and non-book material in the program, personal preparation and presentation, post-program activities and an evaluation report form. Includes a short bibliography.

B. Adolescents

143.   Horner, Beth. "To Tell or Not to Tell: Storytelling for Young Adults." *Illinois Libraries* 65:7 (September 1983): 458-464.

A freelance storyteller and former children's librarian shares insights gained from giving storytelling programs to young adult audiences. Suspense tales, urban belief tales, romantic stories, humorous tales, satires of traditional moral tales, science fiction, and fantasy literature appeal to young adults. When telling to this audience Horner recommends "a straight forward subtle style." Since young adults associate storytelling with young children Horner suggests integrating storytelling into successful existing YA library and school programs and classroom projects that involve participation, such as telling stories to younger children, collecting family stories, or using stories as a springboard to creative writing.

144.   Sutton, Roger. "Telling Tales for YAs." *School Library Journal* 30:3 (November 1983): 44.

Storytelling, like book talks, can lead young adults to more reading, but works best when the recruiting of readers is a secondary goal of the teller. The story and its enjoyment must come first and is most successful when told as from one adult to another as tales have long been done around the world. Sutton discusses several literary tales that work well with adolescents. Many others that are often difficult to tell to young children such as myths, mystical tales, and parodies of traditional tales work well with teenagers who are ready for more complex plots and images. One must select, prepare, and then, says Sutton, simply begin, for telling a story is in many ways just like a book talk except that one gets to tell the end of the story.

C. The Elderly

145.   Johnson, Diane. "Special Report: Storytelling to the Elderly." *Wilson Library Bulletin* 55:8 (April 1981): 593-595.

Little has been written about storytelling to older adults. For this article Johnson interviewed storyteller Michael Burnham about his storytelling activities in senior centers and nursing homes in Cincinnati. Burnham believes that storytelling is a communicative process, not a performance.

"The point of telling stories," Burnham insists,
"is to open a channel of communication, to talk
directly across generational barriers to someone."

D. Outreach Programs

146. Kimmel, Margaret Mary. "Stair-Step Stories."
      Top of the News 23:2 (January 1967): 154-156.

      An example of outreach programs popular in the
      sixties. In cooperation with the Baltimore Urban
      Renewal and Housing Agency, two librarians from
      the Enoch Pratt Free Library conducted summer story
      hours on the front stoops of a run-down neighbor-
      hood. Between 255 and 275 children lived in the
      fifty houses on the block. The children responded
      to the program, choosing books from a large shop-
      ping bag with the Pratt symbol on it for the li-
      brarians to read aloud and listening to stories
      from the oral tradition. At the end of the month
      a reception was held at the neighborhood branch
      library. More than ninety children came and one
      adult couple requested library cards and books.
      Though the results are hard to measure, the li-
      brarians felt the program was well worth their
      time and effort.

147. White, Pura Belpre. "A Bilingual Story Hour Pro-
      gram." *Library Journal* 89 (September 15, 1964):
      3379-3381; *School Library Journal* 11 (September
      1964): 27-29.

      Pura Belpre White became the New York Public Li-
      brary's first Puerto Rican assistant in 1922 when
      a bilingual program of children's services was
      instituted at the 115th Street Branch. Almost
      forty years later (after marriage and several years
      of travel) White returned to the Library in 1961
      as the first Spanish Children's Specialist. Here
      she describes her work with Spanish-speaking chil-

dren and their parents and the programs--story
hours, book talks, puppet shows, etc.--designed
to preserve their cultural background and introduce
them to a new culture.

E. The Handicapped

148. Baskin, Barbara H., and Harris, Karen H. "Story-
telling for the Young Mentally Retarded Child."
In *The Special Child in the Library*. Chicago:
American Library Association, 1976, pp. 114-117.

The emphasis here is on the positive impact of
storytelling on the retarded child's intellectual
development. Pitfalls to avoid in selecting stories are discussed, with examples given of picture
books that work and don't work with mentally retarded children. The article seems a bit heavy
on the *limitations* of such children in contrast
to Luchow's discoveries (see item 153). This article was originally published in *The Journal of
Developmental Disabilities* 1:3 (1975).

149. Brown, Jean D. "Storytelling and the Blind Child."
In *The Special Child in the Library*, edited by
Barbara Holland Baskin and Karen H. Harris. Chicago: American Library Association, 1976, pp. 109-
112.

Brown offers suggestions to storytellers who feel
hesitant about telling to blind children: learning
about the background of the audience, selecting
stories within the blind child's experiential
realm, taping the story as part of preparation,
and the importance of the voice in conveying the
story. She lists thirty-seven stories enjoyed by
blind children (many are picture storybooks in
which the story can be enjoyed without the illus-
trations). This article originally appeared in
The New Outlook 66 (December 1972): 356-360.

150.   Butler, Dorothy. *Cushla and Her Books*. Boston:
       Horn Book, 1975.

       Cushla was born with such severe physical and per-
       ceptual handicaps that her doctors assumed she
       was mentally retarded. Her parents refused to
       accept their diagnosis. They began introducing
       books to Cushla when she was only four months old.
       These story reading experiences had a remarkable
       effect on Cushla's cognitive and social develop-
       ment. By age four she was a happy child and tested
       above average in intelligence. Her inspiring story
       is told by Cushla's grandmother, an educator and
       owner of a specialist children's book store in
       New Zealand.

151.   Champlin, John L., and Champlin, Constance J.
       "Telling Simple Stories with Retarded Adults."
       Catholic Library World 48 (March 1977): 322-327.

       A consultant in mental disabilities and a school
       media specialist urge librarians to organize
       storytelling programs for adults who function at
       or below primary grade level in language use and
       comprehension and have no reading skills. The
       purpose is to increase the adult's ability to
       understand and enjoy literature. Practical ad-
       vice is offered on methods and materials (mainly
       children's books) and participatory activities,
       based on one such project. The teller is advised
       to avoid books in which the main character is a
       child. With this exception, the article is use-
       ful for librarians who tell to mentally retarded
       children.

152.   Huston, Patrick. "Storytelling." In *The Special
       Child in the Library*, edited by Barbara Holland
       Baskin and Karen H. Harris. Chicago: American
       Library Association, 1976, pp. 112-114.

       Stories are to be enjoyed, but for deaf children
       the enjoyment is diminished unless the story has

been structured by the teller. Huston presents
the five steps in structuring: introduction, build-
up, action, reaction, and climax, and offers con-
crete suggestions for each step. This article
originally appeared in *The Volta Review* 74:2 (February 1972): 100-104.

153.   Luchow, Jed P. "Selecting Picture Storybooks for
       Young Children with Learning Disabilities." In
       The Special Child in the Library, edited by Barbara
       Holland Baskin and Karen H. Harris. Chicago: Amer-
       ican Library Association, 1976, pp. 48-51.

       Luchow's study of picture storybooks enjoyed by
       learning disabled children (the list was compiled
       from the responses of forty-four special classroom
       teachers) negates common notions that stories for
       these children must be centered around everyday
       experiences and be concrete and brief. The most
       significant factor, Luchow found, was unity, "ex-
       pressed in oneness of mood, plot, character, har-
       mony between picture and story, or harmony between
       picture and detail." Though learning disabled
       children are often hyperactive and easily dis-
       tracted they can enjoy lengthy books like *Mike
       Mulligan and His Steam Shovel.* Luchow concluded
       that it is not necessary to have specially designed
       books for this group, only more knowledgeable se-
       lection. This article originally appeared in
       Teaching Exceptional Children 4 (1972): 161-164.

154.   Uebelacker, Susan. "Story Hour for the Blind."
       Top of the News 22:4 (June 1966): 414-417.

       Uebelacker recounts her early efforts at providing
       storytelling programs for blind children, her fail-
       ures and successes. Always working with integrated
       groups of blind and sighted children, she found
       shorter tales filled with action and repetition,
       such as "The Gingerbread Boy," were best received.
       Except that jokes and riddles proved to work better

than traditional finger plays between stories,
programs ended up being much the same as other
story programs. Uebelacker concludes that blind
children are children first and blind second, with
all the likes and dislikes of their sighted peers.

155.   Walter, John, and Long, Sarah.   "Story Hours for
       Children with Learning Disabilities."   *Top of the
       News* 35:4 (Summer 1979): 385-388.

       The authors describe a summer story hour program
       for learning-disabled children, sponsored by the
       Public Library of Columbus and Franklin County,
       Ohio.   Twenty-three first to third graders with
       learning disabilities participated in the program
       which was conducted by four librarians.   The li-
       brarians first attended a workshop directed by a
       learning disabilities consultant.   The misunder-
       standings and problems as well as the satisfactions
       connected with the program are noted, thus paving
       the way for other librarians who may wish to carry
       out similar projects.

156.   Werner, Craig.   "A Blind Child's View of Children's
       Literature."   In *Children's Literature*.   Vol. 12.
       New Haven, Conn.: Yale University Press, 1984,
       pp. 209-216.

       Drawing on his childhood memories, a teacher of
       children's literature writes that the stories he
       enjoyed most were those he could perceive through
       tactile means.   These included the "Alice" books
       and the fairy tales of Hans Christian Andersen
       with their long descriptive passages (the Grimm
       tales were too stark).   The need to create pictures
       in the mind in order to make a story come to life
       is necessary for sighted and blind child alike.
       The author concludes that imagination is "the most
       important faculty involved in understanding and
       appreciating a good story."   The best literature
       is based on universal experience and the blind

person is equally able to understand the emotions
it evokes.

F. Family/Home

156A. Birch, Carol L. "Storytelling Programs for the
Family." *National Storytelling Journal* 1:3
(Summer 1984): 14-18.

"Stories were originally intended for adult
audiences and adult sensiblities, though children
listened always, held by the power of the story,
by the teller, and the intimacy of the group.
Unfortunately, storytelling as a shared folk art
for people of all ages has diminished over the
centuries. Yet stories shared with all their
original vitality and virtuality appeal to all
ages, for a good tale, told well, possesses
multiple levels of meaning and accessibility."
In this candid article, Birch relates the obsta-
cles she encountered (and her solutions), story
selection, room arrangement, and publicity for
her program, "The Family Storytelling Hour with
Carol," held monthly over a two-year period at
the Craft and Folk Art Museum in Los Angeles.

157. Chambers, Ruth. "The Fun of Reading Aloud." *Horn
Book* 24:3 (May-June 1948): 177-180.

A parent writes of her pleasure in reading aloud
to her three sons. Though some of the selections
are outdated, the article is worth reading for
its inspiring tone and for citations of problems
posed by publishers for those who read aloud, such
as the practice of running the text across an illustration or where the illustration jumps ahead
of the text.

158. Chase, Mary Ellen. *Recipe for a Magic Childhood*.
      New York: Macmillan, 1953.

      The writer recalls her childhood in Maine during
      the 1890s and the importance of the family reading
      circle in developing her love of literature. This
      essay first appeared in *The Ladies' Home Journal*
      (May 1951).

159. Degh, Linda. *Folktales and Society: Storytelling
      in a Hungarian Peasant Community*. Bloomington:
      Indiana University Press, 1969.

      One of the best studies done of folk literature
      and the community, Degh's work has much to offer
      all who work with folktales, for she examines the
      "correlation of oral folk narratives, their cre-
      ators and performers, and the participant audience
      as a complex whole in the expression of culture."
      Degh begins with a history of the area of Hungary
      that is the center of her study, then goes on to
      the storytelling sessions, specific tellers, and
      their tellings. More than any collection of tale
      texts alone, Degh shares the full story experience
      and offers the storyteller a sense of his place
      as performer in the balance of the community. A
      bibliography and tale type and motif indexes, in
      addition to fascinating information in the col-
      lected notes, conclude the book.

160. Falassi, Alessandro. "Fairy Tales for the Young
      and Old" and "Bedtime and Children's Folklore."
      In *Folklore by the Fireside: Text and Context of
      Tuscan Veglia*. Austin: University of Texas Press,
      1980, pp. 29-104.

      Falassi carefully relates the Tuscan ritualized
      evening gathering of family and friends (Veglia)
      and the interplay of adults, stories, and children.

Adults and children both initially coax their peers
into telling tales including "Cinderella" and "Little Red Riding Hood." A tale may even be told by
several tellers, each giving their version with
an informal discussion of the tale's variants.
As the evening wears on and children begin falling
asleep, the second stage (bedtime folklore) begins
with formula tales, rhymes, and lullabies shared
expressly for children. During the Veglia the
narratives allow the children to "invest all their
emotions in specific and crucial situations and
at the same time introduce them to the inescapable
and omnipresent cultural logic of obligations and
of roles inside of which they would have run their
whole existence."

161. Granzberg, Gary. "TV as Storyteller: The Breakdown
of a Tradition." *Children's Literature Association
Quarterly* 7:1 (Spring, 1982): 18-21.

Storytelling by television has replaced traditional
storytelling in our society with the result that
"children fail to acquire an ability to interpret
the meaning of their experiences within larger,
socially shared traditions and they fail to find
the larger cultural meanings of what they do. Instead, they learn to be alienated and afraid and
perplexed as to their place in the world and their
role in the continuity of culture. They fail to
see the scheme of things and wonder, indeed, if
there's any rhyme or reason to life at all." Anthropologist Granzberg sees a ray of hope in paren-
tal concern about the effects of television and
the growing number of parents who spend more time
reading aloud to their children.

162. Heath, Shirley Brice. "What No Bedtime Story
Means: Narrative Skills at Home and School." *Language in Society* 11:1 (April 1982): 49-76.

Heath, an anthropologist and linguist, studied the

ways in which children from three different socio-
cultural communities in the southeastern United
States learned to use oral and written language.
Children whose parents read to them and made connections between books and "real life" experiences
were more likely to succeed in school. This study
has implications for teachers (and storytellers)
both in their expectations of children's responses
to literature and in their ways of sharing literature with children.

163.   Maguire, Jack. *Creative Storytelling: Choosing,
        Inventing, and Sharing Tales for Children.* New
        York: McGraw-Hill, 1985.

        What Trelease has done for reading aloud Maguire
        attempts to do for storytelling. Maguire has
        taught creative writing and communications and
        written and produced cable television programs.
        He looks on storytelling as a form of communication
        rather than performance. His book is for story-
        telling enthusiasts, for the "average" parent is
        unlikely to keep a word log, take yoga lessons to
        improve breathing, engage in creative writing,
        etc. The text would have benefitted from a nar-
        rower focus and closer editing to eliminate contra-
        dictions and inaccuracies. Nevertheless, Maguire
        has refreshing ideas and an infectious enthusiasm.
        Non-professionals and professionals alike will
        find this engaging reading.

164.   Martignoni, Margaret E. *Family Reading and Story-
        telling.* New York: Grolier Society, 1961.

        Written by a storyteller and former children's
        librarian, this helpful pamphlet answers the why,
        what, who, when, and where of sharing stories and
        poetry aloud within the family. Includes a bib-
        liography.

165. Smith, William Jay. "Rhythm of the Night: Reflec-
      tions on Reading Aloud to Children." *Horn Book*
      36:6 (December 1960): 495-500.

      The title comes from Padraic Colum's belief that
      the quiet sounds of the night (at least in an ear-
      lier period) were conducive to the sharing of sto-
      ries. The poet cites titles especially enjoyed
      with his poet wife, Barbara Howes, and their two
      sons, David, age eleven, and Gregory, age six.

166. van Stockum, Hilda. "Storytelling in the Family."
      Horn Book 37:3 (1961): 246-251.

      The telling of stories to children is vital to
      their literary growth and helpful in general educa-
      tion. Van Stockum believes that trying "to teach
      a child to read who doesn't know the magic of sto-
      ries" is like "trying to catch a fish with an un-
      baited hook." Stories told to a child help develop
      an interest and appreciation for quality language
      and offer the child distilled wisdom and an atti-
      tude toward life, for tales are born out of expe-
      riences of others like ourselves. And beyond all
      else, telling stories is a way for direct interac-
      tion between parent and child, with each giving
      full attention to the other.

167. Wheelock, Lucy. "The Story." In *Talks to Mothers*.
      Boston: Houghton Mifflin, 1920, pp. 108-113.

      Believing stories to be a means of self-discovery,
      self-expression, and self-expansion as well as
      enjoyable, Wheelock discusses the values of parents
      telling stories at home. The child's interest in
      stories is innate and his first connection with
      literature. Yet in their eagerness to impart spe-
      cific information teachers all too often turn the
      story into a didactic lesson rather than allow it
      to be like Froebel's "strengthening bath for the
      mind." It is for this reason that Wheelock so

encourages storytelling in the home where formal
lessons can be left behind and parents can share
the stories they love from lore and their own past
times.

168. Zeitlin, Steven J., Kotkin, Amy J., and Baker,
      Holly Cutting. "Stories for Children." In *A
      Celebration of American Family Folklore: Tales
      and Traditions from the Smithsonian Collection*.
      New York: Pantheon, 1982, pp. 126-145.

      Parents have been telling their children cautionary
      tales and bedtime fantasies for as long as there
      have been parents and children. Here is a sampling
      of stories for children collected under the Smith-
      sonian Family Folklore Program. The collectors
      found that parents adapt traditional tales or in-
      vent new ones to make them more relevant for young
      listener(s) "and to give them an added emotional
      charge."

V. READING ALOUD

Children who are not spoken to by live and responsive adults will not learn to speak properly. Children who are not answered will stop asking questions. They will become incurious. And children who are not told stories and who are not read to will have few reasons for wanting to learn to read.

Gail E. Haley
1971 Caldecott Medal
acceptance speech

169. Dolman, John, Jr. *The Art of Reading Aloud*. New York: Harper, 1956.

One of the best books available on the art of reading poetry aloud. Dolman, a teacher of speech, play production, and oral reading, distinguishes between speaking, reading, and acting. Reading aloud is communicative thought-sharing. The reader must think in images and rhythmic movements. Dolman offers sound technical advice, illustrated by numerous examples. Includes an appendix of poems for reading aloud.

170. Kimmel, Margaret Mary, and Segel, Elizabeth. *For Reading Out Loud!: A Guide to Sharing Books with Children*. Foreword by Betsy Byars. New York: Delacorte Press, 1983.

Two master teachers of children's literature write about the values of reading aloud, how to find time to read aloud, and how to read aloud. They list and annotate 140 titles appropriate for reading aloud to children from kindergarten age through eighth grade. The annotated entries give a short summary of the plot, advice on deletions, suggested listening level, and length of the reading segments. The compilers caution against reading aloud books, such as those by Judy Blume, that "explore experiences and feelings that are personal and not intended to be shared between adults and children." Picture books are not included on the list because the emphasis is on listening (not illustration) and, because poetry "deserves a list of its

own," only a few poetry anthologies are cited.
Cross-listings by subject, length, type, and settings are a helpful feature. The selections reflect the authors' wide knowledge of books and
children's reading interests.

171. Laughton, Charles. "Storytelling." *Atlantic
      Monthly* 185 (June 1950): 71-72.

The versatile British actor relates how he became
a storyteller and gives advice to those who want
to learn to read aloud well. "... they must learn
to seek the response in someone else's eyes as
they read ... the whole thing is bound up in wanting to communicate something you like to others
and have them like it too." This piece was written
at the completion of Laughton's successful run of
fifty-two performances of storytelling to American
audiences.

172. Lewis, Claudia. "The Pleasant Land of Counter-
      pane." *Horn Book* 42:5 (October 1966): 542-547.

The writer's thoughts on coming across a book from
childhood are an antidote to the notion that children need simplified versions. Her early exposure,
through hearing literature read aloud by her story-
loving mother, to words and concepts not fully
understood "had the power to generate vortexes of
feelings that swirled up through life and are not
completely distinguished.... A child's ability
to visualize people and places, as a story unfolds,
may be at its keenest in these early years, when
all the senses are sharp and receptive. For the
child, the story world takes on an immediate and
vivid reality similar to the reality of the world
of play. And since his lively emotions are always
trigger-poised to take the leap into personified
form, he himself becomes the doer, the slayer,
the runner, the weeper. In short, as he listens,
he is not merely hearing a story; he is living an

intensified life spread out for him in new dimensions of time and place." Lewis recommends several books for teachers to read aloud. Crucial to selection are "the adult's own excitement over the story" and a version with words to savor.

173. McGillis, Roderick. "Calling a Voice Out of Silence: Hearing What We Read." *Children's Literature in Education* 15:1 (1984): 22-29.

We participate in a literary text "only when its rhythm comes to life, when we hear it." Adults who read aloud can bring life to a text that the child may lose as he learns to read privately. "Private reading is silent reading, and silent reading leads to ... reading in monotone.... Each text speaks in its own voice, and we must call this voice out of the silence of academic and private reading if we are to save our readers and our texts." A persuasive argument for sharing literature orally.

174. Trelease, Jim. *The Read-Aloud Handbook*. New York: Penguin, 1982. Revised edition, 1985.

With the zeal of an evangelist and the common touch of a newsman, Trelease is a most persuasive advocate of reading aloud to children. In this revision of his bestseller, the author discusses the need to read aloud to children, when and how to do it, and how to cope with the pervasive influence of television. The second half of the book, the Treasury of Read-Alouds, is an annotated bibliography of recommended titles to read aloud, from picture books to novels, based on first-hand experience.

175. Willcox, Isobel. *Reading Aloud with Elementary
      School Children*. Englewood Cliffs, N.J.: Prentice-
      Hall, 1963.

      Addressed to teachers, this helpful pamphlet offers
      suggestions on what to read, how to prepare chil-
      dren for the listening experience, scheduling,
      the classroom setting, and appropriate post-reading
      activities. The emphasis throughout is on literary
      pleasure: "however serious the purpose of reading
      aloud to children, and whatever educational contri-
      bution it can make, the goal will not be achieved
      unless the element of delight is present."

176. Wilner, Isabel. "Making Poetry Happen: Birth of
      a Poetry Troupe." *Children's Literature in Educa-
      tion* 10:2 (Summer 1979): 86-91.

      Her mother introduced her to *Mother Goose* and *A
      Child's Garden of Verses*; her father read aloud
      The Book of Common Prayer. From these early ex-
      periences Wilner developed a passionate love of
      poetry and a desire to share it with children.
      As librarian of the campus elementary school at
      Towson State University, Baltimore, Maryland, she
      created "a poem troupe" (the children named it
      after the mime troupe that visited their school).
      Wilner and the children read poems to other groups
      of children, children's literature classes, classes
      on the teaching of reading, and classes in language
      arts. Since then Wilner has nurtured many poetry
      troupes and compiled an anthology of poetry to
      read aloud, *The Poetry Troupe*. Her article in-
      cludes a bibliography of recommended poetry col-
      lections for children.

VI. STORYTELLERS

... traces of the storyteller cling to the story the way the handprints of the potter cling to the clay vessel.

Walter Benjamin
Illuminations

177. Azadovskii, Mark. *A Siberian Tale Teller,* translated by James R. Dow. Austin: University of Texas
Press, 1974.

Convinced that storytelling is a complex act and
involving far more than text alone, Azadovskii
worked with various tellers to find the interrela-
tionship among environment, personality of teller,
and the text of the tale. Just as writers vary,
some being more poetic, fantastic, or realistic,
so do tellers, with each one subtly emphasizing
what that person sees as most important. And just
like the writer, the teller is also faced "con-
sciously or unconsciously, [with] the same assign-
ment as the creative writer: the arrangement of
his materials, choosing and shifting the latter,
and the formulation of his artistic intention."
Azadovskii's primary source was Vinokurova, a
fifty-year-old illiterate female who took obvious
pride and pleasure in her storytelling abilities.
Her personal style was always to try to bring
folktale-like surroundings close to actual reality
and she was more interested in custom and psychological elements than magical events. Yet, regardless of style, "the individual mastery of the
narrator comes out most clearly in the structure
and character of the dialogue" which reflects his
personality and creative senses. This study was
first published in German in 1928 as Folklore Fel-
lows Communications No. 68.

178.   Baker, Augusta. "Once Upon a Time." In *Come*
        Hither!, edited by Lawrence Clark Powell. Los
        Angeles, Calif.: Yeasayers Press, 1966, pp. 9-14.

        Augusta Baker relates how she became a storyteller,
        beginning with the stories she heard from her
        grandmother during childhood. This paper was one
        of four read at a farewell meeting for Frances
        Clarke Sayers upon her retirement from library
        service and teaching, held at the University of
        California at Los Angeles on June 12, 1965.

179.   Britton, Jasmine. "Gudrun Thorne-Thomsen: Story-
        teller from Norway." *Horn Book* 34:1 (February
        1958): 17-28.

        This reminiscence of a storyteller "in the great
        tradition" reveals the source of her magic: a me-
        ticulous use of words, the cadence of a beautiful
        voice, a masterly use of the pause, a sense of
        drama, a love of literature, and a belief in the
        power of stories. Britten covers Thorne-Thomsen's
        family background and her training to be a teacher,
        her work at the University of Chicago's Laboratory
        School and the storytelling program in the field
        houses of the Chicago playgrounds, her principal-
        ship of the Ojai Valley School near Santa Barbara,
        California, her lectureships in library schools,
        and her storytelling records and books for chil-
        dren. A section of the article prepared by Helen
        Fuller and Jane Bradley, two librarians who par-
        ticipated in a storytelling class taught by Thorne-
        Thomsen, presents the storyteller's philosophy
        and advice on learning and telling stories.

180.   Campbell, Marie. *Tales from the Cloud Walking*
        Country. Bloomington: Indiana University Press,
        1958.

        In addition to collecting and editing an excellent
        anthology of tales from eastern Kentucky, Campbell

has included brief, but telling character sketches
of her six informants. Her descriptions of appear-
ance, voice, manner of telling, and quotes from
the tellers not only enhance the tales by providing
them with a vibrant context, but offer an interesting comparison of storytelling styles and thematic
preferences. Settings for the tellings are briefly
related and in the passage on Uncle Tom Dixon,
Campbell includes a marvelous anecdote of a child
literally learning to become a storyteller at someone's knee and how she was influenced in regard
to style and pacing. A bibliography of sources
and comparative tales is included.

181.   Cech, John. "Breaking Chains: Brother Blue, Story-
       teller." *Children's Literature*. Vol. 9. New
       Haven, Conn.: Yale University Press, 1981, pp.
       151-177.

       An insightful portrait of Hugh Morgan Hill, better
       known as Brother Blue, based on information gath-
       ered from newspapers, magazine articles, and Blue's
       six-page resume of degrees, awards, performances,
       and personal interviews. Blue graduated cum laude
       from Harvard with an A.B. in Social Relations.
       He also holds a M.F.A. from the Yale Drama School.
       Since 1968, following the slaying of Dr. Martin
       Luther King, Blue has made a fulltime commitment
       to storytelling, taking his art to the streets,
       hospitals, schools, and churches of the community.
       A highly improvisational storyteller, Blue incor-
       porates "the energy of black art forms and lan-
       guage, along with modern dance, music and theatre
       into the mainstream of the storytelling tradition."
       Blue says: "I try to work like a jazz musician,
       blowing an old song from my SOUL, but blowing it
       ever new." His free style and "weird" costume
       repel some, spellbind others. Behind the mask of
       the performer Cech found "a soft-spoken, deeply--
       even painfully--sensitive individual. The chains
       in the title refer to slave chains loaned to Blue
       by his professor of American Church History at
       Harvard.

182.   Comstock, Sarah.   "New York's Story Lady."   *Amer-
       ican Magazine* 77 (February 1914): 68, 70.

       A contemporary account of Anna Cogswell Tyler,
       first supervisor of storytelling at the New York
       Public Library, and her remarkable ability to in-
       terest West Side gang member children in litera-
       ture: "The art that holds a room breathless is
       hers to the finger tips."   Ms. Tyler organized
       storytelling clubs which met weekly and at which
       the children told or read stories to one another.
       At the time of the article there were twenty-two
       girls' clubs and twenty boys' clubs in the library
       system; storytelling was carried out in thirty-six
       of the library's branches with more than 38,000
       children attending the over 1600 "entertainments."

183.   Dorson, Richard.   "Oral Styles of American Folk
       Narrators."   In *Folklore: Selected Essays*.   Bloom-
       ington: Indiana University Press, 1972, pp. 99-146.

       As the focus of folktale telling evolves to include
       performance as well as text, Dorson discusses the
       ways body, voice, gestures, facial expression,
       and the whole human presence contribute to a tell-
       ing.   His own field work having taken him many
       places in the United States, Dorson describes var-
       ious folk narrators and their styles, including a
       Yankee lobster fisherman, a French-Canadian auto-
       mechanic, a Swedish lumberjack, and Southern-born
       Blacks who had moved north to an all-Black farming
       town.   All are different and all outstanding.
       Dorson includes texts to seven tales told by his
       informants and concludes the article with an ex-
       amination of Abraham Lincoln as a masterful folk
       narrator.

184. English, Gladys. "A Storyteller Visits Califor-
      nia." *Horn Book* 21 (November-December 1945): 468-
      471.

      A warm reminiscence of Gudrun Thorne-Thomsen's
      visit to California in the spring of 1945 and her
      talks on storytelling. By then a grandmother and
      "retired," Mrs. Thorne-Thomsen continued to inspire
      librarians and teachers to interpret literature
      to children through the art of storytelling.

185. Jordan, Alice M. "The Cronan Story Hours in Bos-
      ton." *Horn Book* 26:6 (November-December 1950):
      460-464.

      The head of children's work at the Boston Public
      Library pays tribute to the Cronan family of story-
      tellers, Mr. and Mrs. Cronan and Mrs. Cronan's
      sister, Mrs. Margaret Powers. Writing at a time
      when the Cronans were still carrying out their
      work in libraries and schools all over the city,
      Jordan notes: "the accord reached by a united fam-
      ily group in touch with each other's methods and
      daily experiences with the children's responses,
      no less than the continuity of the art they have
      long pursued, make storytelling in Boston a pecu-
      liar tradition."

186. McCloskey, Margaret Durand. "Our Fair Lady!"
      Horn Book 41:5 (October 1965): 481-486.

      A personal portrait of storyteller Ruth Sawyer by
      her daughter. Family celebrations, rituals, and
      pastimes, with Sawyer starring as fisherwoman,
      blueberry picker, cook, gardener, and mother, are
      recounted with warmth and humor. This issue of
      the *Horn Book* also includes Mother Mary Cecile's
      speech presenting the Regina Medal to Ruth Sawyer
      on April 20, 1965, and Ruth Sawyer's acceptance
      speech on the occasion of receiving the Laura
      Ingalls Wilder Award on July 6, 1965.

187.   Moore, Anne Carroll.   "Ruth Sawyer, Story-teller."
       Horn Book 12:1 (January-February 1936): 34-38.

       Anne Carroll Moore recollects her first meeting
       with Ruth Sawyer--"a story-teller with the gift
       of song, a courageous heart, and a sheaf of stories
       freshly gathered in Donegal." She describes
       Sawyer's telling of "The Voyage of the Wee Red
       Cap" to forty dolls "and as many children born of
       Irish and Italian parents" at the Hudson Park
       branch of the New York Public Library in 1910.
       This was the beginning of a Christmas tradition
       and Sawyer's long association with the Library.

188.   Sawyer, Ruth.   *My Spain: A Storyteller's Year of
       Collecting*.   New York: Viking, 1967.

       At the age of twelve Ruth Sawyer fell in love with
       Spain through the stories of Washington Irving.
       "Half a lifetime later" she went in search of her
       own Spain and to gather stories to tell to American
       children. Her zestful account of that year gives
       a feeling for the land and people of Spain and
       for the storyteller herself.

189.   Sayers, Frances Clarke.   "A Skimming of Memory."
       Horn Book 52:3 (June 1976): 270-275.

       Frances Clarke Sayers recalls her student days at
       the Carnegie Library School during World War I.
       She gives a vivid description of the faculty, many
       of whom became noted in the profession. Not to
       be missed is her description of Gudrun Thorne-
       Thomsen who came from Chicago to give a three-week
       course in storytelling--"when she told a story,
       it was like watching a tree grow; you felt it com-
       ing from such roots!" A memorable article.

190. Stewart, Barbara Home. "The Folktellers: Shehera-
     zades in Denim." *School Library Journal* 25:3 (No-
     vember 1978): 17-21.

     As times change so do the varieties of storytell-
     ers, styles of telling, and places stories are
     told. Stewart traveled with Barbara Freeman and
     Connie Regan and shares with enthusiasm their
     work as freelance professional storytellers in
     places as different as public libraries and
     street corners in Manhattan. "It's a different
     kind of storytelling we do," says Regan, "than
     what you'd hear on a back porch. It's changed a
     bit, once it's delivered from a stage and behind
     a microphone, but it is still very personal."
     By studying from master tellers in the field and
     doing workshops and programs across the country,
     the two tellers, who enjoy their work, hope to
     help restore people's ability to visualize.

191. Wolkstein, Diane. "An Interview with Harold
     Courlander." *School Library Journal* 20:9 (May
     1974): 19-22.

     Harold Courlander, novelist and folklorist, is a
     specialist in African and Afro-American cultures.
     His collections of folktales from these and other
     non-European peoples were published in the forties,
     fifties, and sixties, and are still valued by
     storytellers for their authenticity and direct
     style. Diane Wolkstein, a writer, storyteller,
     and admirer of Courlander, interviews him about
     his methods of collecting story material and the
     basis for his selection (personal liking).
     Courlander is bothered by the Gothic element in
     many traditional European tales and thinks "the
     folklore of non-European cultures has much to give
     us, both adults and children." He sees folklore
     and oral literature "as a way towards understanding
     thoughts and values of non-Western peoples....
     Moral values are basically the same.... Customs
     and traditions are developed as particularized

human responses to deal with environmental and
other realities."

VII. THE BUILDING OF BACKGROUND

It is a matter of years, of a lifetime, this
building of background for storytelling, for
it is a matter of growth. Something one must
never hurry through but be continuously aware
of and eager for. Something to which one
must bring a keen appetite, fresh enthusiasms,
an integrity of attitude, a clear-burning
zeal. To be ever ready to discard that which
one can no longer use with honesty. To put
together all one gathers that there may be a
final authority in the telling and a dignity
and truth in what one has to tell--this is
of the utmost importance. For as storytellers we are concerned not alone with
amusement, or with education, or with dis-
traction; nor is it enough to give pleasure.
We are concerned with letting a single
stream of light pass through us as through
one facet of the gem or prism that there may
be revealed some aspect of the spirit, some
beauty and truth that lies hidden within the
world and humankind.

Ruth Sawyer
*The Way of
the Storyteller*

192. Applebee, Arthur. *The Child's Concept of Story:*
Ages Two to Seventeen. Chicago: University of
Chicago Press, 1978.

Using studies done at the University of London,
Applebee examines the child's cognitive development
with regard to story. Plentiful examples demonstrate the child's growing and expanding concept
of story from nonsense sounds through disjointed
episodes to plotted stories. As the child develops
so does his ability to separate fact and fantasy.
His relationship to fiction expands as he is able
to enjoy stories that are further and further from
immediate experience. Listening to one story several times helps the young child, for he "relies
on poetic techniques, re-experiencing the story
in the process of retelling it." Of special interest is Applebee's method of distinguishing
progressingly developed narrative forms: heaps,
sequences, primitive narratives, unfocused chains,
focused chains, and, finally, narratives in which
each incident not only develops out of the previous
one, but also adds new levels to the primary theme.

193. Cameron, Eleanor. *The Green and Burning Tree: On*
the Writing and Enjoyment of Children's Books.
Boston: Little, Brown, 1962.

This collection of twelve essays, some previously
published in slightly different form, is a classic
to be read and re-read for enjoyment and enlighten-
ment. The title comes from the author's essay on
time fantasy. Cameron, a highly respected writer

of children's literature, shows appreciation of
the writer's craft and respect for the child audience. Though the focus is on *writing,* storytellers
will be enriched by Cameron's insights into the
work of such authors as Hans Christian Andersen,
Beatrix Potter, and Eleanor Farjeon, as well as
individual books by numerous others.

194.   Carlson, Ruth Kearney, editor. *Folklore and Folk-
        tales Around the World*. Newark, Del.: Interna-
        tional Reading Association, 1972.

        A compilation of ten papers presented at the Inter-
        national Reading Association's fifteenth annual
        convention held in Anaheim, California, in 1970.
        The focus of the conference was on folktales of
        oral and literary tradition and the use of such
        tales with school age children. There is an ex-
        tensive bibliography of folktale collections, ar-
        ranged by geographic area. The articles include:
        "World Understanding through the Folktale," by
        Ruth Kearney Carlson; "Latin American Folklore
        and the Folktale," by Genevieve Barlow; "Anglo-
        Celtic Lore in America," by Richard Chase; "Re-
        flections and Distortions: Canadian Folklore as
        Portrayed in Children's Literature," by Sheila A.
        Egoff; "The American Hero in American Children's
        Literature," by Rosemary Weber; "Russian Folklore
        and the Skazka," by Miriam Morton; "The Scandina-
        vian Folktale," by Norine Odland; "Finnish Folk-
        lore and the Finnish Folktale," by Taimi M. Ranta;
        "Some Folktales and Legends from Northern England,"
        by John D.A. Widdowson; and "Tales and Legends
        from Micronesia," by Hector H. Lee.

195.   Clarkson, Atelia, and Cross, Gilbert. *World Folk-
        tales: A Scribner Resource Collection*. New York:
        Scribner's, 1980.

        While this collection contains over sixty tales
        from around the world, its strongest points are

its scholarship and cross-references. Believing
that the best way to study a tale is by reading
several variants, the authors cite several parallel
stories for each tale as well as principal motifs,
tale types, and "Notes and Comments." Of particular interest to those working with children is an
appendix on use of folktales in the classroom which
discusses the integration of tales in reading,
social studies, art, dramatics, and creative writing. A sample comparative paper on one tale by a
fourth grade student is included, in addition to
a project outline and suggestions for teachers.

196. Cook, Elizabeth. *The Ordinary and the Fabulous:
An Introduction to Myths, Legends and Fairy Tales
for Teachers and Storytellers*. Cambridge: Cambridge University Press, 1969. Second edition,
1976.

For Cook, "a grown-up understanding of life is
incomplete without an understanding of myths, legends, and fairy tales." Here she discusses the
what, how, and where of introducing the fabulous
in the classroom. Cook's critical analysis of
parallel passages from different versions of stories, such as Gawain's journey to the castle of
the Green Knight, are an invaluable aid to the
storyteller. The text has not been materially
altered in the second edition but the annotated
booklist has been revised and enlarged. In the
preface to the second edition Cook cites societal
changes that have favored myth and fable and those
that have been destructive. She takes a skeptical
view of a new genre--the romance for teenagers
built upon plots taken from myth, legend, and fairy
tales and treated in a novelistic manner.

197. Cox, Miriam. "Japan and Greece Meet in Myth."
Horn Book 44:1 (February 1968): 40-47.

Cox (to whom we are indebted for her study of

"Cinderella" variants) here draws attention to
the similarities and differences in motifs and
worldviews in Greek and Japanese mythologies.
Among the similarities are the Japanese "Divine
Producing Goddess" who gives birth to "Little
Prince Renown" from her finger as Zeus produced
Athena from his head; Kumeno, the Japanese Icarus,
and a Japanese goddess who cannot return to her
husband because, like Persephone, she has eaten
food in the underworld. The Greeks and the Japanese are both sensitive to beauty, but the concept
that all nature is invested with divine spirit is
central to Japanese mythology whereas the Greek
gods are more closely tied to human affairs. Another striking difference is the absence in Japan
of a rich repository of *pourquoi* stories found in
Greek mythology.

198.   Degh, Linda. "Folk Narrative." In *Folklore and
       Folklife,* edited by Richard Dorson. Chicago: Uni-
       versity of Chicago, 1972, pp. 53-83.

       The impulse to tell and listen to stories is innate
       in man and the range of stories in the oral tradi-
       tion alone is large. Degh discusses the basic
       history of folktale study from early emphasis
       solely on text to the present, where the teller
       and setting are equally appreciated. "Rooted in
       their social environment, stories are extremely
       sensitive to group and individual attitudes; the
       greater their popularity, the greater their in-
       consistency.... As long as they are told, they
       vary, merge, and blend; a change in their social
       value often results in a switch into another
       genre." There are, however, basic forms and for-
       mulas that give structure to folk literature and
       Degh provides an excellent overview of types and
       genres ranging from myths to the oral retelling
       of television shows.

199. Degh, Linda. "Grimm's *Household Tales* and Its
      Place in the Household: The Social Relevance of a
      Controversial Classic." *Western Folklore* 38:2
      (April 1979): 83-103.

      Long the best-known collection of folktales in
      the western world, the Grimm tales are far from
      the folk purity which many once believed them to
      be, yet remain vital elements in contemporary
      times. Degh discusses the manner of the Grimms'
      collecting, their sources (some non-German), and
      the eventual retelling of many tales into a stan-
      dardized text. When first published, the collec-
      tion's introduction urged caution in sharing with
      children. And though there are few of the tales
      that are truly appropriate for household story-
      telling to children, the tales have been kept alive
      primarily by children and their caregivers. The
      tales have been praised and condemned, used as
      Nazi propaganda, bastardized in print, and trans-
      formed into film and television, yet they continue
      to satisfy, for "society's need for magic tales
      seems to be fulfilled by the remarkably modest
      but active and persistent repertoire selected from
      the Grimm tales."

200. de la Mare, Walter. "Introduction." In *Animal
      Stories*. New York: Scribners, 1939, pp. xiii-lvi.

      In addition to exploring the historical background
      of animal tales and their anthropomorphic relation-
      ship to humans, de la Mare poetically describes
      our ongoing bond with folktales. "As with loved
      and valued old friends, we need never weary of
      sharing them again, and of enjoying all they are
      and mean to us. They come--like dew; they go--
      like hoarfrost; and they come again--like the
      nightingale." Nor is this just in terms of joyful
      stories, for tales of sorrow equally feed the imag-
      ination, strengthening the heart and helping us
      see ourselves more clearly.

201. Dundes, Alan, editor. *Cinderella: A Casebook.*
      New York: Garland, 1982.

      The eminent folklorist has set high standards in
      his scholarly but readable anthology of essays
      about "Cinderella." Freudian, Jungian, structural-
      ist, and other approaches are presented, covering
      a time period of more than one hundred years. The
      inclusion of three versions of "Cinderella"
      (Basile, Perrault, Grimm) and a selected bibliog-
      raphy for further research add to the value of
      this outstanding work.

202. Dundes, Alan. "Folklore as a Mirror of Culture."
      Elementary English 46 (1969): 471-482.

      Dundes views folklore as autobiographical ethnology
      (people's own descriptions of themselves) and be-
      lieves it has much to offer anyone who wants to
      learn about one's own and others' cultures. Folk-
      lore allows the study of other peoples from the
      inside out, focusing on special concerns of the
      people and the universality of those concerns. As
      folklore exists everywhere, Dundes encourages the
      teacher to begin with the children's own playground
      and family lore. This establishes the variants
      of folklore; the why and how such variants exist
      can be discussed later. Believing that one cannot
      learn about folklore from books, Dundes, a leading
      folklorist, includes several example projects and
      samples of lore that one might use with students,
      including folk anecdotes about teachers and stu-
      dents.

203. Eberhard, Wolfram. "Notes on Chinese Story Tell-
      ers." *Fabula* 11 (1970): 1-31.

      Historically, it was common for Chinese story-
      tellers to use prompting books that supplied basic
      story outlines. Studying three contemporary tell-
      ers, Eberhard finds the same still exists, for

tellers use stories of heroic tales that, over
time and use, become folk property. The tellers
rarely read the text, but do keep it nearby for
plot reference as they expand or shorten the story
and translate it into more colloquial speech using
intonation to heighten the drama. Literature has
long been viewed in a nonconcrete manner in China.
"The written or printed form is not final but tem-
porary or preliminary, valid at a certain time
for a certain kind of audience. It is a living
story which changes and develops continuously,
and the storyteller is the agent of change. He
tells the story as he feels his audience likes to
hear it." And at any given time a new retelling
may appear in print much as the endless adaptations
of "Hansel and Gretel" in the United States. Both
teller and audience in China are solidly aware of
the constant evolution in folk literature.

204. Evans, W.D. Emrys. "The Welsh Mabinogion: Tellings
and Retellings." *Children's Literature in Education* 9:1 (Spring 1978): 17-33.

Evans' main criterion in evaluating translations
and retellings of the medieval Welsh tales is how
well they read aloud. The author's familiarity
with the Mabinogion, which he shares with readers
who know little about the work, and his comparisons
of different retellings make this valuable background reading for the storyteller. Of the many
translations and retellings cited, Evans has high
praise for Lady Charlotte Guest's nineteenth-
century translation and Jeffrey Gantz's recent
one, as well as Evangeline Walton's retellings.
Evans also discusses works based on the Mabinogion,
such as Lloyd Alexander's "Chronicles of Prydain"
and Alan Garner's *The Owl Service.*

205. Halpert, Herbert. "Folktales in Children's Books:
      Some Notes and Reviews." *Midwest Folklore* 2:1
      (Spring 1952): 59-71.

      Recognizing that the "responsible folklorist cannot
      afford to overlook the folktale collections which
      are published as children's books," Halpert notes
      collections by Harold Courlander and Richard Chase
      as valuable examples of high quality. Courlander
      provides basic (if not extended) resource notes
      which are valuable to both documentation and the
      child's understanding of the story. Such notes
      and introductions help the child experience the
      context of the story as well as the text. The
      artificial context created by Chase for his col-
      lection, in which more and more people gather dur-
      ing an all-night storytelling session, creates
      another problem, for it presents a situation that
      rarely occurs. Others, including Jagendorf, use
      folktales as seeds for the writing of new folk-
      like stories, about which Halpert has no disagree-
      ment as long as they are presented as such, rather
      than as pure folktales, and are judged by literary
      rather than folklore standards.

206. Howard, Elizabeth Fitzgerald. "Collecting Folk-
      tales in Northern Nigeria." *Top of the News* 41:1
      (Fall 1984): 85-87.

      A teacher of children's literature found herself
      with a unique opportunity of living out the folk-
      lore section of her course when she accompanied
      her Fulbright professor-husband to northeastern
      Nigeria. Here she relates with charm her experi-
      ence as a listener of traditional tales that con-
      tinue to be told and to have meaning for present-
      day Nigerians.

207. "Jack Tales Issue." *North Carolina Folklore Journal* 26 (September 1978).

As some of the core stories in United States folk literature, the Jack Tales have a long tradition in family storytelling. This feature issue includes both retellings and essays on their telling and contents: "Jack and the Heifer Hide" by Marshall Ward, "Cat 'n Mouse" by Marshall Ward, "Jack and the Three Steers" by Ray Hicks, "Whickity-Whack" by Ray Hicks, "The Jack Tale: A Definition of a Folk Tale Sub-Genre" by C. Paige Gutierrez, "The Narrative Style of Marshall Ward, Jack Tale-Teller" by C. Paige Gutierrez, "The Literary Unity of Ray Hicks' Jack Tales" by W.H. Ward, and "Jack as Archetypal Hero" by Charles T. Davis.

208. Jacobs, Leland B., editor. *Using Literature with Young Children*. New York: Teachers College Press, 1965.

A collection of twelve short articles by educators about various ways of using literature with children, including but not limited to storytelling and reading aloud. The emphasis throughout is on enjoyment of literature and the teacher as a model in the literature experience. Among the contributors are Leland Jacobs, Kay Vandergrift, Shelton T. Root, Jr., Charles Reasoner, and James E. Higgins.

209. Jakobson, Roman. "Commentary." In *Russian Fairy Tales*, collected by Aleksandr Afanas'ev. New York: Pantheon, 1945, pp. 631-651.

Like so many other people, rich Russians viewed the ability to read printed literature as a status symbol elevating them above the nonliterate peasants, yet their desire for folktales remained so strong they would hire storytellers to entertain their families. Jakobson discusses the gradual

process of collecting the tales in print via translation and Afanas'ev's approach to his work and
its quality. While Afanas'ev believed the personality of the teller was reflected in the telling,
he felt that within the folklore hierarchy the
tale always comes first, noting a need for caution
in both telling and collecting. Jakobson also
touches on the varying changes and influences on
Russian folktales due to writers' interests in
retelling them, as many have, for artistic and/or
political re-interpretation.

210.   Lasser, Michael. "Weaving the Web of Story: Arche-
        type and Image as the Bearers of the Tale." *Chil-
        dren's Literature in Education* 10:1 (Spring 1979):
        4-10.

        Using three traditional tales--Gail E. Haley's *A
        Story, A Story,* Jan Carew's *The Third Gift,* and
        the Grimms' "The White Snake"--Lasser demonstrates
        that imagery "makes the story not only possible,
        but, for its own duration, and thereafter in the
        reader's imagination, believable as well."

211.   Lewis, C.S. "On Three Ways of Writing for Chil-
        dren." In *Only Connect: Readings on Children's
        Literature.* New York: Oxford University Press,
        1969, pp. 207-220. (Reprinted from the *Proceedings*
        of the Bournemouth Conference, 1952).

        Writers of children's stories approach their work
        in three ways: "find out what they (children) want
        and give them that, however little you like it
        yourself"; write with a particular child in mind
        (to whom the story has already been told); write
        a children's story "because a children's story is
        the best art-form for something you have to say."
        Within his essay Lewis argues convincingly for
        the child's access to fairy tales. "... fairyland
        arouses a longing for he knows not what. It stirs
        and troubles him (to his lifelong enrichment) with

the dim sense of something beyond his reach and,
far from dulling or emptying the actual world,
gives it a new dimension of depth."

212. Lord, Albert B. *The Singer of Tales*. New York:
      Atheneum, 1965.

      Lord explores the oral tradition of song and nar-
      rative with respect and scholarship. Specifically
      dealing with Yugoslavian epic singers, Lord's dis-
      coveries and theories extend to all areas of story
      singing and storytelling. The book's first section
      examines "Singers: Performance and Training" and
      "Writing and Oral Tradition" as well as those
      areas dealing with themes and formulas. Believing
      that the goal of the oral tradition is stability
      of essential story rather than exact wording of
      text, Lord discusses the oral tradition as a con-
      tinually evolving art form where, unlike most
      others, the work is composed and performed at the
      same time. Lord sees the goal of quality story-
      telling to be "the preservation of tradition by
      the constant re-creation of it."

213. Luthi, Max. *The European Folktale: Form and Na-
      ture,* translated by John D. Niles. Philadelphia:
      Institute for the Study of Human Issues, 1982.

      First published in German in 1947 Luthi's study
      of the European folktale is a masterful examination
      of what he calls the lasting truths of tales. In
      exploring the tales from both their inner structure
      and their outer relationship to teller and lis-
      tener, Luthi provides a fuller view of storytelling
      as he refracts different theories off one another.
      "A folktale can be interpreted, but any single
      interpretation will impoverish it." As the first
      form of poetic expression, the folktale offers
      much, yet demands nothing. "It does not interpret
      or explain: it merely observes and portrays. And
      this dreamlike vision of the world ... accepts

itself so matter-of-factly and is given verbal
expression so unerringly that we let ourselves be
carried away by it in a state of bliss."

214. Luthi, Max. *Once Upon a Time: On the Nature of
      Fairy Tales,* translated by Lee Chadeayne and Paul
      Gottwald. New York: Frederick Ungar, 1970.

      Exploring elements of all tales as he discusses
      specific titles, Luthi considers all aspects of
      tales as a literary art form. "The psychologist,
      the pedagogue knows that the fairy tale is a fun-
      damental building block and an outstanding aid in
      development for the child; the art theorist per-
      ceives in the fairy tale--in which reality and
      unreality, freedom and necessity, unite--an arche-
      typal form of literature which helps lay the ground
      work for all literature, for all art." Luthi ex-
      amines the elements of maturation, symbolism,
      style, meaning, form, and the image of man in fairy
      tales and, in turn, their place in our lives. As
      unreal, but not untrue, fairy tales reflect the
      conditions of our existence and may function as a
      personal slayer of inner dragons through our shar-
      ing of them.

215. McVickar, Polly Bowditch. "Storytelling in Java."
      Horn Book 40:6 (December 1964): 596-601.

      McVickar gives a vivid description of a night of
      storytelling in Java (from nine o'clock in the
      evening until six the next morning). Using tradi-
      tional shadow puppets and accompanied by music,
      the dalang performed the adventures of Rama and
      his beautiful wife, Sita. The writer, an American
      who lived in Indonesia for two years, conveys to
      the reader all the enchantment of the occasion.

216. Neumeyer, Peter F. "The Child as Storyteller: Teaching Literary Concepts Through Tacit Knowledge." *College English* 30:7 (April 1969): 515-517.

The author, a professor at Harvard and a father, relates a domestic incident (in which his son attempts to resolve a story Neumeyer is creating) as proof of Polanyi's theory of tacit knowledge. Human beings, even the very young, know that stories do resolve and that they have form. The challenge for teachers of literature is to use the child's tacit knowledge of storytelling to teach literary concepts.

217. Nodelman, Perry M. "What Makes a Fairy Tale Good: The Queer Kindness of 'The Golden Bird.'" *Children's Literature in Education* 8:3 (Autumn 1977): 101-108.

Acknowledging that folktales predate current literary conventions, Nodelman applies these current conventions to folktales as a means of discovering their unique qualities apart from other genres. At every level the folktale fails standard conventions of quality, yet remains fascinating and often beautiful because of how it works against them. Fairy tales stress an acceptance of the unusual and once one accepts what appears to be illogical he can learn to discern the logic in it, trust its operations, and believe in new ways. "If a child's view of the world is always shifting in response to new strange things, then he will find the world described in fairy tales very satisfying; particularly when fairy tales insist by their very lack of astonishment that acceptance is possible, and that being shocked by experience and not understanding it can be enjoyable.... For children, the world of fairy tales may be an accurate image of their real world."

218.   Norton, Eloise Speed, editor. *Folk Literature of*
        the British Isles: Readings for Librarians, Teach-
        ers and Those Who Work with Children and Young
        Adults. Metuchen, N.J.: Scarecrow Press, 1978.

        Norton has gathered a broad range of essays dealing
        with British folk literature, its content and use
        in contemporary literature. Of particular interest
        to the storyteller are: "Memories of My Father,
        Joseph Jacobs" by May B. Hays, "Stories and Story-
        telling in Ireland" by Kevin Danaher, "Story-
        telling in Ireland" by Padraic Colum, and "Folk-
        lore--One Writer's View" by Mollie Hunter. While
        most of the essays can be found in separate jour-
        nals, their gathering here forms a valuable aid
        in regard to British tales told both there and in
        the United States.

219.   Opie, Iona, and Peter Opie, editors. *The Classic*
        Fairy Tales. London: Oxford University Press,
        1974.

        Twenty-four of the best-known fairy tales as they
        were first published in English. A general intro-
        duction and the introductory sections for each
        tale provide the storyteller with historical back-
        ground, changes in the tale over the years, and
        parallels in other cultures.

220.   Phinney, Alice. "Children and Stories in Iran."
        Horn Book 44:6 (December 1968): 718-722.

        An American who taught English-as-a-second-language
        in the girls' schools of Kerman, Iran, during 1966
        and 1967 gives a fascinating glimpse of young women
        in a mid-Eastern culture and their reactions to
        western European and American literature. The
        examples given include "Cinderella," the story of
        John Alden and Priscilla, and "The Merchant of
        Venice." Phinney also gives examples of Persian
        folklore, including two stories about Mullah Nasr-
        ed-din.

221. Propp, Vladimir. *Morphology of the Folktale.* Second edition, revised and edited with a preface by Louis A. Wagner and a new introduction by Alan Dundes. Austin, Tex.: University of Texas Press, 1968.

Propp analyzed Russian folktales in terms of functions, i.e., actions, rather than characters. His work demonstrated that folktales employ a similar pattern and that events occur in a logical sequence. His approach can be used to study other European folktales.

222. Robinson, Evelyn R., editor. *Readings About Children's Literature.* New York: McKay, 1966.

A collection of more than sixty articles by authorities in the field. Part 7 includes several articles of interest to the storyteller, including "Fairy Tales and Their Effects Upon Children," by Ruth C. Horrell; "Traditional Scandinavian Literature for Children," by Siri Andrews; "Memories of My Father, Joseph Jacobs," by May Bradshaw Hays; and "American Folk Tales," by Mary Gould Davis.

223. Saxby, Maurice, editor. *Through Folklore to Literature.* Sydney: IBBY Australia Publications, 1979.

This anthology of fourteen papers first presented at an Australian Conference of IBBY in 1978 is organized into chapters entitled "Origins," "Universals," "Cultural Voices," and "When Cultures Meet." The essays include viewpoints and scholarship from around the world with five of particular interest to storytellers: "The Impulse to Story" by Edward Blishen, "Ritual in Oral Tradition" by Anne Pellowski, "Young and Growing: The Uses of Story" by Patricia Scott, "Story Traditions in Australia Aboriginal Cultures" by Jack Davis, and "When Cultures Meet: A Writer's Response" by

Patricia Wrightson. Each contributor in his own
way offers supportive and enlightening evidence
to Blishen's statement that "the impulse to tell
stories, and hear them, and retell them, and improve them or worsen them, according to our gifts,
is a fundamental element in our being human."

224.   Smith, Lillian. *The Unreluctant Years*. Chicago:
       American Library Association, 1953.

       Written by the head of library work with children
       at Toronto, this book has become a classic on the
       evaluation of children's literature. Ms. Smith's
       critical approach is a helpful guide for selecting
       the best versions of fairy tales, myths, and hero
       tales for sharing with children.

225.   "Storytelling and Education Issue." *Parabola* 4:4
       (1979).

       An outstanding issue including stories and essays
       on storytelling, puppetry, and stories' influence
       on people. "As the Twig Is Bent" provides a fas-
       cinating dialogue between Waldorf teacher Anne
       Charles, Montessori teacher Nancy Rambusch, and
       teacher/artist Richard Lewis on the interrelation-
       ship of story and child. Also included is James
       Hillman's essay "A Note on Story: A Jungian Point
       of View on the Significance of Story." Article
       after article expands the world of story, including
       a review of a play about the Baal Shem-Tov by the
       Traveling Jewish Theater that begins by stating:
       "Stories go in circles. They don't go in straight
       lines. So it helps if you listen in circles be-
       cause there are stories inside stories and stories
       between stories and finding your way through them
       is as easy and as hard as finding your way home.
       And part of the finding is the getting lost. If
       you're lost, you really start to look around and
       to listen."

226. Stott, Jon C. "In Search of the True Hunter: Inuit
      Folktales Adapted for Children." *Language Arts*
      60:4 (April 1983): 430-438.

      Scott compares stories about Inuits written by
      Inuits and non-Inuits. The non-Inuit often makes
      literary assumptions that are not appropriate and
      presents the culture inaccurately. For example,
      in *The Day Tuk Became a Hunter* Melzak links land
      and sea animals in a way that would have been taboo
      among the Inuits. Other authors soften the cru-
      elty, violence, and terror found in many Inuit
      folktales. Stott argues that one of the best ways
      to help children develop sensitivity to other cul-
      tures is "to let them read or hear the stories
      children of these other cultures would have been
      familiar with." Teachers (and storytellers) should
      present stories from other cultures with sympathy
      and insight.

227. Tatar, Maria. "Tests, Tasks, and Trials in the
      Grimms' Fairy Tales." In *Children's Literature*.
      Vol. 13. New Haven: Yale University Press, 1985,
      pp. 31-48.

      Tator looked at two different types of heroes in
      Grimms' tales--the "happy-go-lucky simpleton" and
      the "roguish trickster" for common character traits
      and predictability of plots. The two types are
      closer than they appear at first. The trait that
      sets the simpletons apart is compassion. Once
      the simpleton passes the test of compassion he is
      assisted in his tasks by helpers (whom the hero
      has helped), and through his trials the hero gains
      strength and courage to defeat his enemies. Male
      and female protagonists are treated differently
      in these tales--"Fairy tale heroes receive gifts
      and assistance once they actively prove their com-
      passion and humility; heroines, in contrast, become
      the beneficiaries of helpers and rescuers only
      after they have been abased and forced to learn
      humility." Fearless heroes, such as the "Coura-

geous Tailor," rely on their own mental and physical resources and are, therefore, closer to trick-
sters. Tator discovered that "inversion of character traits, violation of narrative norms, and
reversal of conditions" are characteristic of the
fairy tale. It is their psychological truths that
remain stable and "endow all fairy tales with a
special charm and magic."

228. Tedlock, Dennis. *The Spoken Word and the Work of
      Interpretation*. Philadelphia: University of Penn-
      sylvania Press, 1983.

      This anthology of sixteen essays explores specifi-
      cally the world of Zuni oral narrative, but with
      implications for all who work collecting, trans-
      lating, or retelling folktales. Tedlock sees the
      speaking storyteller not as a "writer who fears
      to make use of the shift key, but an actor on a
      stage" with the sound and pacing as vital as the
      words he speaks. Chapters of special interest
      to storytellers are: "On the Translation of Style
      in Oral Narrative," "Learning to Listen: Oral His-
      tory as Poetry," "Ethnography as Interaction: The
      Storyteller, the Audience, the Fieldworker and
      the Machine," and "The Story of How a Story Was
      Made." The book concludes with an excellent bib-
      liography of related readings.

229. Thompson, Stith. *The Folktale*. New York: Holt,
      1946.

      This primary resource for anyone working with folk-
      tales and storytelling centers on an overview of
      folk literature by culture and form. Of special
      value is the text's detailed indexing by tale type
      and motif and the bibliography of core collections
      of tales arranged by culture. Thompson concludes
      by discussing the theories and classification of
      folktales and the folktale as a living art. While
      the main elements of a tale seem set within each

cultural area, there are elements of variation.
The storyteller of quality is careful to retain
the traditional forms and formulas while adding
his own verbal style and manner of telling. Long
the main form of entertainment around the world,
Thompson believes storytelling will continue to
offer artistic expression to the imagination. His
final statement, while positive in tone, seems to
exclude much of what contemporary psychologists
have been exploring. Stating that tales "will
long continue to be one of the chief means of fur-
nishing education and solace to unlettered men
and women," Thompson seems to see no educational
connection or source of solace in tales for liter-
ate children and adults.

230. Tolkien, J.R.R. "On Fairy-Stories." In *Tree and
Leaf*. Boston: Houghton, 1964.

Believing that there is value in fairy stories
for adults as well as children, Tolkien discusses
and explores the basic questions of "what," "from
where," and "why" of tales. His questions and
his theories in response are complex, but enlightening, especially when he comes to compare the
origin of stories to the origin of language and
the mind. Tolkien believes that both inheritance
and independent invention contribute to the web
of story as it is passed on through generations.
As such, tales of the faerie (not just fairies
and spirits) are ever changing and are "by no means
rocky matrices out of which the fossils cannot
be prised except by an expert geologist. The ancient elements can be knocked out, or forgotten
and dropped out, or replaced by other ingredients
with the greatest ease: as any comparison of a
story with closely related variants will show."

231. "The Trickster Issue." *Parabola* 4:1 (1979).

From Hopi and Zuni clowns to the fool of the Tarot

to the Hodja, the role of the trickster in traditional societies is to transmit spiritual truths
through the techniques of shock and humor. Among
the articles in this fascinating issue are those
in which Joseph Epes Brown talks about Black Elk,
the great Sioux Medicine Man; David Leeming reflects on the wisdom of Nasr-ed-din, "the wisest
of fools"; and P.L. Travers inquires into the concept of the youngest brother.

232.   "Using Folktale Films." *Young Viewers* 5:1 & 2.
        (Winter/Spring 1982): 2-40.

        This entire issue is a model guide to the use of
        Tom Davenport's film, *The Frog King or Faithful
        Henry*. The issue includes activities related to
        different objectives and for three different age
        groups: kindergarten to 4th grade, 5th-8th grade,
        and 9th-12th grade; bibliographies on "Filmmaking
        and Film Use," "Animals, Animals in Art, Besti-
        aries," "Folktales and Folklore Resources," "His-
        tory Resources," and "Poetry"; a Filmography, and
        reviews of films related to *The Frog King* in theme
        or aspects of folklore. A unique resource.

233.   Walker, Barbara K. "The Folks Who Tell Folk Tales:
        Field Collecting in Turkey." *Horn Book* 47:6 (De-
        cember 1971): 636-642.

        A folklorist, Walker discusses her efforts at col-
        lecting folktales in Turkey and the adapting of
        some of them for publication as children's books
        in the United States. Working to find the best
        tellers and most authentic Turkish tales, Walker
        found "the more unschooled a storyteller was, the
        more natural and effective his storytelling and
        the more representative it was of tale telling in
        rural Turkey." Each teller she recorded told in
        a different style and responded differently to
        physical setting and the process of being recorded.
        While some were eager to tell, others had to be

coaxed by others telling first and setting the
mood. In translating and adapting the narratives
Walker found Howard Pyle a good model with his
use of "robust conversation and an ample use of
native proverbs."

234. Walley, Irene. "The Cinderella Story 1724-1919."
In *The Signal Approach to Children's Books,* selected by Nancy Chambers. Metuchen, N.J.: Scarecrow Press, 1980, pp. 140-155.

A discussion of the various editions of "Cinderella" found in the National Art Library, Victoria
and Albert Museum. Though the emphasis is on
changes in illustration, the article also notes
changes in the story line from Perrault's succinct
version (1724) to George Cruikshank's elaborate
retelling (1854) in which he inserts a temperance
tract, to C.S. Evans' full-length novel (1919).
Such changes reflect the social period as well as
the reteller's personal imprint.

235. Willard, Nancy. "Well-Tempered Falsehood: The
Art of Storytelling." In *Angel in the Parlor:
Five Stories and Eight Essays.* San Diego: Har-
court, 1983, pp. 222-239.

Poet and Newbery Medalist Nancy Willard recalls
her storytelling games as a child and explores
the connections between telling stories, writing
stories, and hearing them. Keeping in mind that
the original goal of telling stories was to entertain (all levels: Grimm to Kafka), Willard discusses the poetic economy of folktales to show
the direct telling style of the narrator and how
telling and listening to stories comes to posi-
tively affect one's writing. Stories may be formed
of falsehoods and the writer's job may be to tell
a lie, "but in the telling to make it true."

236.   Wilson, Anne. "Magical Thought in Story." *Signal*
        36 (September 1981): 138-151.

        Wilson explores the differences among magical
        thinking, imaginative thinking, and rational think-
        ing. Magical thought is wholly free from the laws
        and realities of the external world and focused
        exclusively on the inner world of the protagonist.
        What appear to be absurdities in the traditional
        folktales and the works of individual writers "make
        good sense if they are seen as the creation of
        the hero and heroine." Wilson illustrates her
        theory with a discussion of Grimm's tale of "The
        Golden Bird" and Daphne du Maurier's *Rebecca*. Such
        works have a characteristic structure (fantasy
        structure) and include repetitive, patterned ac-
        tivities; conflicting emotions which propel the
        story forward from a dissatisfying initial situa-
        tion to a satisfying solution, use of magical words
        or objects, and disguises. Magical fantasy com-
        bines immediate appeal with emotional nourishment.

237.   Wolkstein, Diane. "Introduction." In *The Magic
        Orange Tree and Other Haitian Folk Tales*. New
        York: Knopf, 1978.

        More than simply an introduction to the specific
        stories in the collection, Wolkstein writes vividly
        of storytelling in Haiti and of the place of the
        storyteller in Haitian society. The text of the
        story is vital; the most entertaining and charis-
        matic tellers did not necessarily have the best
        worded texts and some less proficient performers
        had the more poetic texts. Wolstein discusses
        this range of telling quality and styles showing
        that telling folktales is a multi-leveled art form.
        Also of value is her background information on
        Haitian culture which is not only a benefit for
        those reading the stories, but an outstanding ex-
        ample of contextual field work.

238. Zipes, Jack. *Breaking the Magic Spell: Radical Theories of Folk and Fairy Tales*. Austin: University of Texas Press, 1979.

While agreeing that folk and fairy tales can offer much insight and enjoyment, Zipes believes they can lead one toward confusion if one fails to attend to their history and how to evaluate their potential. Zipes combines folk literature and literary fairy tales in his scope and deals primarily with societies' absorption with the literary fairy tale. One of the few to apply political theories to this genre and storytelling, Zipes provides thought provoking chapters entitled "Might Makes Right--The Politics of Folk and Fairy Tales" and "The Instrumentation of Fantasy: Fairy Tales, the Culture Industry and Mass Media." Zipes concludes with a critical discussion of Bettelheim's *The Uses of Enchantment,* stating that: "The categorical imperative used by Bettelheim constantly prevents him from achieving his purpose of uncovering the significance of folk tales for child development.... Everything remains in Bettelheim's own realm of reified Freudian formulas which restrain the possibilities for a vital interaction between the tale and the child and between the adult and the child."

VIII. BIBLIOGRAPHIES AND INDEXES

The story's done, the end has come, but
somewhere it goes on and on.

Gyula Illyes
Once Upon a Time:
Forty Hungarian Folk-Tales

239. Aarne, Antti. *The Types of the Folk-Tale: A Classification and Bibliography,* translated by Stith Thompson. New York: Lenox Hill, 1928.

Though perhaps frustrating to some because many of the sources cited are either rarely available or are in non-English languages, Aarne's index is *the* source for all tale type identification of folktales. Divided into three broad categories of animal tales, ordinary tales, and jokes and anecdotes, this index is valuable in providing form and order to the variety of folk patterns and helping one find variants of core tales in different cultures.

240. American Library Association, Children's Services Division. *For Storytellers and Storytelling: Bibliographies, Materials, Resource Aids.* Chicago: American Library Association, 1978.

A brief pamphlet listing books, excerpts from books, articles, recordings, film, and videotape on storytelling and containing a bibliography of sources of stories.

241. Cathon, Laura, editor. *Stories to Tell Children: A Selected List.* Eighth edition. Pittsburgh: University of Pittsburgh Press for Carnegie Library of Pittsburgh, 1974.

The latest edition of a list first published in 1906. Stories are listed for three age groups and for ten holidays.

242.   Coughlan, Margaret N. *Folklore from Africa to
       the United States: An Annotated Bibliography.*
       Washington, D.C.: Library of Congress, 1976.

       As African peoples were forcibly moved from their
       homes to North America, their folktales traveled
       with them and were, in time, recreated to suit
       their new surroundings and emotional needs. Cough-
       lan's selective, yet still expansive, bibliography
       includes collections of tales gathered in Africa,
       the West Indies, and the United States, thus making
       its 190 titles a fine resource for exploring the
       evolution of tales as well as a vital source for
       African and black folk literature for retelling.
       The index is by title of collection and author-
       collector.

243.   Cox, Miriam. *Cinderella: Three Hundred and Forty-
       Five Variants.* Introduction by Andrew Lang. Lon-
       don: Folk-lore Society, 1893.

       Cox, a folklorist, exhibits the universality of
       the tale with her abstracts of 345 variants ar-
       ranged under three headings: "Cinderella," "Cat-
       skin," and "Cap o' Rushes."

244.   Eastman, Mary Huse. *Index to Fairy Tales, Myths
       and Legends.* Boston: Faxon, 1926. Supplement
       1937. Second supplement 1952.

       These three volumes are primary entries to folk-
       tales published for children in English in the
       first half of the twentieth century. Though or-
       ganization differs a little between the first and
       last two volumes, the access to information is
       consistent. Tales can be found by title with all
       sources listed for each tale and variant titles,
       by subject (though not extensive), and by geo-
       graphical and ethnic origin. Books analyzed are
       also indexed by author/compiler and title.

245. Hardendorff, Jeanne B. *Stories to Tell: A List of Stories with Annotations*. Fifth edition. Baltimore, Md.: Enoch Pratt Free Library, 1965.

    Special features of this list include sections on picture books for television storytelling and suggested story hour programs.

246. Haviland, Virginia. *Children's Literature: A Guide to Reference Sources*. Washington, D.C.: Library of Congress, 1966.

    The sections "Storytelling" and "Folktales, Myths, and Legends" in this guide and in the first supplement to the guide (1972) are of invaluable aid to the storyteller.

247. Hunt, Mary Alice, editor. *A Multimedia Approach to Children's Literature*. Third edition. With a Foreword by Ellin Greene. Chicago: American Library Association, 1983.

    "A Selective List of Films (and Videocassettes), Filmstrips, and Recordings Based on Children's Books." Useful for the librarian or teacher planning multimedia programs for children. Out-of-print materials are not included, but may be found in library collections. Therefore, the second edition, edited by Ellin Greene and Madalynne Schoenfeld, is still a valuable tool for the program planner. Both editions include a bibliography of related readings, selection aids, program aids, and realia, as well as a section on authors and illustrators in the non-print media.

248. Iarusso, Marilyn. *Stories: A List of Stories to Tell and to Read Aloud*. Seventh edition. New York: New York Public Library, 1977.

    An annotated list of stories enjoyed by children

in the story hours held at the New York Public
Library. This list was first compiled in 1927 by
Mary Gould Davis and is continually updated by
the library's storytelling specialist. In addition
to the listing of individual stories there are a
section of poems and stories for reading aloud, a
list of storytelling recordings, and a subject
index, including a section of folktales by geo-
graphical area.

249.   Ireland, Norma Olin. *Index to Fairy Tales, 1949-
       1972, Including Folklore, Legends and Myths in
       Collections*. Westwood, Mass.: Faxon, 1973.

       Covering four hundred folktale collections, this
       index is a primary source for those seeking par-
       ticular tales or variants of a given tale. Indi-
       vidual tales are indexed by title, country of or-
       igin, and major subjects within the tale. "See
       also" entries help assure the user of finding the
       desired stories despite variant titles. Designed
       to supplement the early tale indexes done by
       Eastman, this volume covers collections published
       between 1949 and 1972.

250.   Ireland, Norma Olin. *Index to Fairy Tales, 1973-
       1977, Including Folklore, Legends and Myths in
       Collections*. Westwood, Mass.: Faxon, 1979.

       Indexed by subject and title, this supplementary
       volume to Ireland's initial *Index to Fairy Tales,
       1949-1972* covers 130 collections published in the
       years 1973-1977. Both volumes are of great as-
       sistance to anyone working with folktales and chil-
       dren.

250A. Kohn, Rita. *Mythology for Young People: A Ref-
       erence Guide*. New York: Garland, 1985.

       Adults who work with children will find this an-

notated bibliography of mythologies a very useful
tool. Entries are arranged by subject and within
each subject by author. Among the more than fifty
subjects are African Mythology, American Mythology
(subdivided by regions), Greek Mythology, Indic
Mythology, Norse Mythology, Animals in Mythology,
and Stars in Mythology. "Encountering Mythology,"
an introductory essay by Carl J. Wenning, Director
of the Illinois State University Planetarium, seems
fitting since the sky held a special place in mythology. Wenning suggests ways for parents and
teachers to encourage the child's sense of wonder.
He emphasizes the oral tradition and the role of
the storyteller in preserving ancient truths.
There is an Author/Illustrator Index and the annotations indicate the age audience for each entry.

251.   Leach, Maria, editor. *Standard Dictionary of Folk-
       lore, Mythology and Legend*. New York: Funk and
       Wagnalls, 1949.

       This two-volume set, written by a group of out-
       standing scholars from related disciplines, is a
       rich source for basic information concerning all
       areas of folklore from motifs and specific cultures
       to characters and phrases. Most entries are cross-
       referenced and frequently include titles useful
       for specific culture or language rather than using
       current political boundaries or groupings.

252.   MacDonald, Margaret Read. *The Storyteller's
       Sourcebook: A Subject, Title and Motif Index to
       Folklore Collections for Children*. Detroit: Neal-
       Schuman/Gale Research, 1982.

       This major aid to all who work with folktales and
       children indexes 556 folktale collections and 389
       picture books listed in *Children's Catalog,* 1961-
       1981, and *Booklist,* 1960-1980. MacDonald provides
       the first access through the standard motif index
       as established by Thompson and the tale types es-

tablished by Arrne and Thompson. Especially valuable is the detailed ethnic and geographic index
which acknowledges specific cultures rather than
merely countries and continents. The work is based
on the author's dissertation at the Folklore Institute and the Graduate Library School at Indiana
University.

253.   Power, Effie L., editor. *Lists of Stories and
Programs for Story Hours,* compiled by the staff
of the Children's Department, St. Louis Public
Library. White Plains, N.Y.: Wilson, 1915.

An important early bibliography for the storyteller. Entries are arranged by age categories:
3 and 4, 5 and 6, 7 to 9, and for cycle story hours
for older children. Also includes stories for
holidays and selections for reading aloud. Of
historical interest.

254.   Preschool Services and Parent Education Committee,
Association for Library Service to Children, ALA.
*Opening Doors for Preschool Children and Their
Parents.* Second edition. Chicago: American Li-
brary Association, 1981.

An annotated bibliography of picture books (arranged by type) and nonprint materials suitable
for use with young children. The list was compiled
by librarians working with preschool children and
their parents.

255.   Ramsey, Eloise. *Folklore for Children and Young
People: A Critical and Descriptive Bibliography
for Use in the Elementary and Intermediate School.*
Philadelphia: American Folklore Society, 1952.

Combining scholarship and popularism, Ramsey provides a fine core bibliography designed for anyone
working with folklore and children. Materials

cited show solid folklore scholarship as well as
being suited to the taste of children. Volumes
included were selected for children's self-reading
and as resource collections for teacher-tellers.
Of added value to storytellers are the sections
on rhymes, games, and literary extensions which
have much material that can be included in story
programs.

256. Rooth, Anna Birgitta. *The Cinderella Cycle*. New
York: Arno Press, 1980. (Reprint of the 1951 edition published by Gleerup of Lund, Sweden, which
was originally presented as the author's thesis,
University of Lund, 1951.)

Based on Miriam Roalfe Cox's investigation of the
Cinderella tale. The intention of Ms. Cox's work
was to group the known variants into types. Rooth
investigated the relationship among the types of
Cinderella tales and their dissemination. From
her study of approximately 300 tales in addition
to the 345 in Cox's study she concluded that Type
A ("One Eye, Two Eyes, Three Eyes") originated in
the East. Type AB developed in the Near East from
Type A and an Oriental motif-complex. Type B (the
Cinderella tale proper) developed in southeastern
Europe from Type AB and spread throughout Europe.
Type C (male protagonist) evolved in the Near East
as an equivalent of Type A and migrated first to
southeastern Europe, whence it reached Ireland
and Scandinavia. Rooth analyzes the differences
between the European and Oriental traditions and
discusses the motifs and motif-complexes found in
the types and their variants. This scholarly work
is an invaluable resource for the storyteller interested in the evolution of a tale from simple
composition into a more artistic whole and the
relationship between different cultures that it
reveals.

257.   Shannon, George W.B. *Folk Literature and Children:
       An Annotated Bibliography of Secondary Materials.*
       Westport, Conn.: Greenwood Press, 1981.

       Since the invention of printing, adults have de-
       bated as to whether or not folktales are suitable
       for children. Writers, educators, and psycholo-
       gists have each in their own way explored, con-
       demned, and/or praised the folktale with general
       opinion changing in cycles of twenty some years.
       Organized by primary perspective (literature, ed-
       ucation, and psychology), this bibliography of
       more than 450 entries stretches chronologically
       from John Locke to the early 1980s and in form
       from journal essays to monographs and sections of
       books. With author, title, and subject index this
       work is of solid use for anyone wanting to explore
       the complex interrelationships between children
       and the stories they hear.

258.   Thompson, Stith. *Motif Index of Folk Literature:
       A Classification of Narrative Elements in Folk-
       tales, Ballads, Myths, Fables, Mediaeval Romances,
       Exempla, Fabliaux, Jest-Books and Local Legends.*
       Bloomington, Ind.: Indiana University Press, 1955.

       This detailed classification of images, situations,
       plot twists, and forms provides an invaluable en-
       trance into the interweaving patterns of folk lit-
       erature around the world. Consisting of five vol-
       umes, a related bibliography, and a volume-sized
       subject index, Thompson's work is of continual
       importance to all storytellers.

259.   Toothaker, Roy E. "Folktales in Picture-Book For-
       mat: A Bibliography." *Library Journal* (April 15,
       1974): 1188-1194.

       A selective and annotated bibliography of folktales
       in picture book format chosen with the storyteller
       in mind. The folktales are from fifty-three coun-
       tries around the world.

260. Ullom, Judith C. *Folklore of the North American Indians: An Annotated Bibliography.* Washington, D.C.: Library of Congress, 1969.

A selective bibliography, the criteria used being "(1) statement of sources and faithfulness to them, (2) a true reflection of Indian cosmology, and (3) a written style that retains the spirit and poetry of the Indian's native manner of telling." The tales represent eleven culture areas: Eskimo, Mackenzie, Plateau, North Pacific, California, Plains, Central Woodland, Northeast Woodland, Iroquois, Southeast, and Southwest.

APPENDIX

A. Films/Videotapes on Storytelling

By Word of Mouth ... Storytelling in America. National Association for the Preservation and Perpetuation of Storytelling, 1983. Videotape--3/4" or 1/2" VHS or Beta. color. 58min.

A documentary featuring nationally known storytellers as they performed at the Tenth National Storytelling Festival in Jonesborough, Tennessee. The film, narrated by NAPPS founder Jimmy Neal Smith, was the Silver Electra Award winner of the 1984 Birmingham International Educational Film Festival.

Jay O'Callahan: A Master Class in Storytelling. Vineyard Video Productions, Inc., 1983. 16mm. color. 33min. Also available in videotape.

O'Callahan, a well-known modern bard who tells stories of his own creation as well as traditional tales, talks about the importance of storytelling in communication and its meaning to our lives in a technological society. He proceeds to mesmerize viewers with his theatrical style of telling, assuming a different voice for each character, and a manner that ranges from whimsical to dramatic. This film took first prize in teacher education at the National Educational Film Festival, 1985.

The Pleasure Is Mutual: How to Conduct Effective Picture Book Programs. Westchester (New York) Library System, 1966. 16mm. color. 24min.

An award-winning film produced by William Stoneback and Joanna Foster of Connecticut Films for the Westchester Library System. Portions of ten picture book programs in libraries, day care centers, and playgrounds are shown, with the children unaware of the camera for the most part. The script covers selection of books for picture book programs, how to present picture books to groups of children, the skills needed by the teller, and the rewards of such programs.

The Power of Stories. Commonwealth Schools Commission, Australia, 1984. Produced and written by Ursula Kolbe. Directed by Tom Zubrycki. Distributed by Weston Woods. 16mm. color. 17min.

An exceptionally fine training film featuring Maurice Saxby, Clare Scott-Mitchell and Robbie Wilson of the Sydney College of Advanced Education in a discussion of the function of stories in child development. The camera moves back and forth between the academic discussion and shots of children listening to their teachers reading aloud. Pauline Brailsford's reading of the award-winning picture book, *John Brown, Rose and the Midnight Cat,* by Jenny Wagner and illustrated by Ron Brooks, is memorable.

Reading Aloud: Motivating Children to Make Books into Friends, Not Enemies. 16mm. color. 80min. Available for rental from Reading Tree Productions, 51 Arvesta Street, Springfield, Massachusetts 01118.

"Reading Aloud" is the next best thing to hearing Jim Trelease in person. The dynamic lecturer talks about the importance of reading aloud and "sustained silent reading," the problem of television, and how

he successfully weaned his children from the tube
after four months of tears! Trelease keeps his
viewers listening as he demonstrates his expertise
with a humorous rendering of *Ira Sleeps Over*. In
the second half of the film he talks about the books
themselves, always emphasizing the pleasure to be
found in them. The film closely follows the text
of *The Read-Aloud Handbook* and proves why Trelease's
book is a bestseller.

Storytelling. Lesson 13 in series, Jump Over the
Moon: Sharing Literature with Young Children. Co-
produced by the South Carolina ETV Network and the
University of South Carolina, 1982. Videotape.
color. 30min.

Host Rick Sebak interviews Augusta Baker,
Storyteller-in-Residence at the University of South
Carolina and formerly the Coordinator of Children's
Services at the New York Public Library. Mrs.
Baker, a renowned storyteller, discusses the art
and technique of storytelling, talks about story
hours at the New York Public Library, and delights
a group of school children with her telling of an
"Uncle Bouqui" story.

A *Storytelling Sampler*. Massachusetts Board of
Library Commissioners, 1981. Videotape. color.
24min.

Written and narrated by Richard Ashford. The tape
includes portions of stories being told to groups
of adults and children by storytellers Richard
Ashford, Ellen Block, Gisela Lehovec, and Laura
Pershin. The tape was a joint project of the
Jordan-Miller Storytelling Committee--a section of
the Massachusetts Library Association and the New
England Round Table of Children's Librarians, and
the Massachusetts Board of Library Commissioners.
For a copy, send request with a blank 30-minute
videotape (3/4", 1/2" BETA, 1/2" VHS or open reel)

to Richard Taplin, Non-Print Media Unit, Commonwealth of Massachusetts Board of Library Commissioners, 648 Beacon Street, Boston, Massachusetts
02215.

There's Something About a Story. Connecticut Films,
Inc., 1969. 16mm. color. 27min.

Produced by Joanna Foster and William D. Stoneback
for the Dayton and Montgomery County Public Library.
The film shows ten storytellers with different
styles and varying degrees of experience. They are
not professional storytellers but librarians, teachers, and parents in Dayton, Ohio. They talk about
the joy of sharing stories with children, what it
means for children to hear stories, and how to select and prepare a story. Three complete stories
and parts of seven others are told in various set-
tings--libraries, a boys' club, classrooms, a scout
meeting, a park, and a museum.

B. Storytelling Recordings

Charlotte's Web. Pathways of Sound, 1970. (POS
1043) 8s. 12in. 33rpm.

E.B. White reads aloud his beloved book, chapter
by chapter.

Eli Wallach Reads Isaac Bashevis Singer. Miller-
Brody Productions, 1973. (NAR 3063/64) 4s. 12in.
33rpm.

Tales from *Zlateh the Goat and Other Stories* and
When Schlemiel Went to Warsaw and Other Stories.

Elsie Piddock Skips in Her Sleep: Stories and Poems by Eleanor Farjeon. A Gentle Wind, 1984. (GW 1025) Cassette.

Ellin Greene reads poems by Eleanor Farjeon and tells three Farjeon tales: "Elsie Piddock Skips in Her Sleep," "Nella's Dancing Shoes," and "The Sea-Baby."

Eva LeGallienne Reads Hans Christian Andersen. Miller-Brody, 1973. (L-504-509) 6 cassettes.

The famous actress uses her own translations in this reading of eight Andersen tales: "The Emperor's New Clothes," "The Princess and the Pea," "The Tinderbox," "The Happy Family," "It's Absolutely True!," "Thumbelina," "The Steadfast Tin soldier," and "The Ugly Duckling."

Fairy Tale Favorites, Vol. I and Vol. II. CMS Records, Inc., 1970. (CMS 593, 595) 2 records. 12in. 33rpm.

Told by Mary Strang. Vol. I includes "The Sleeping Beauty," "Little Red Riding Hood" (original French version), and "Cinderella." Vol. II includes "The Nightingale," "The Steadfast Tin Soldier," "The Princess on the Pea," and "The Fairies" (Toads and Diamonds).

Folk Tales from West Africa. Folkways/Scholastic Records, 1959. (7103) 2s. 10in. 33rpm.

Harold Courlander reads five tales from his collection, *The Cow-Tail Switch*: "The Cow-Tail Switch," "Younde Goes to Town," "Talk," "Throw Mountains," and "Don't Shake Hands with Everyone."

Folk Tales Retold. American Library Association, 1970. 8 cassettes.

These tapes were originally produced by RCA-Victor on 78rpm for the American Library Association. Contents: "Baldur," "Gudbrand-on-the-Hillside," "Tales from the Volsunga Saga," and "Sleeping Beauty," told by Gudrun Thorne-Thomsen; "Brer Mud Turtle's Trickery," told by Frances Clarke Sayers; "The Frog," and "Schnitzle, Schnotzle, Schnootzle," told by Ruth Sawyer; and "A Paul Bunyan Yarn" and "A Pecos Bill Tale," told by Jack Lester.

Folktales and Legends from Great Britain. CMS Records, 1972. (CMS 633) 2s. 12in. 33rpm or cassette.

Tales from England, Ireland, Scotland, and Wales, selected from the BBC's Jackanory storytelling program for children. Contents: "Cap of Rushes," told by Lee Montague; "The Giant's Wife," told by Maureen Potter; "The Faery Flag of Dunvegan," told by Magnus Magnusson; "Where Arthur Sleeps," told by Ray Smith. The versions were specially written for telling on radio.

Frances Clarke Sayers, Storyteller. Weston Woods, 1966. (WW 705, 706) 4s. 12in. 33rpm.

A noted librarian-storyteller tells stories by Carl Sandburg and Hans Christian Andersen.

The John Masefield Story-telling Festival. Toronto Public Library. 6s. 12in. 33rpm.

Highlights from the festivals held in 1961, 1966, and 1972. Among the storytellers are Augusta Baker, Eileen Colwell, Rita Cox, and Alice Kane.

Joy to the World. Weston Woods, 1968. (WW 707)
2s. 12in. 33rpm.

Ruth Sawyer narrates three stories and a poem from
her book of the same name. The selections include
"The Two Lambs," "This Is the Christmas," "The Pre-
cious Herbs of Christmas," and "A Carol from an
Irish Cabin."

Miami Storytelling Festival. Ann Arbor, Mich.:
Audio-Visual Education Center, University of Michi-
gan, 1956. Audio tapes.

A recording of the Storytelling Festival sponsored
by the Children's Services Division of the American
Library Association and held at the ALA Conference
in Miami Beach, June 1956. Among the eleven storytellers recorded are Augusta Baker, Eileen H.
Colwell, and Frances Clarke Sayers.

*Padraic Colum Reading from His Irish Tales and Po-
ems.* Folkways, 1966. (FL 9737) 2s. 12in.
33rpm.

Side 1: "Blarney Castle" from *Cross Roads in Ireland*
and "The Wizard Earl" from *Big Tree of Bunlahy.*
Side 2: Selections from *Collected Poems,* with a few
remarks before the reading of each poem.

Pearl Primus' Africa. Miller-Brody, 1971. (P-
601-3) 3 cassettes.

Storyteller-anthropologist Pearl Primus presents
traditional folktales, legends, and proverbs of
Africa, interwoven with songs and the drums.

Perez and Martina. CMS Records, 1966. (CMS 505)
2s. 12in. 33rpm. and cassette.

Pura Belpre reads a traditional Puerto Rican folktale and a favorite with children. (Side 1, English; side 2, Spanish.)

*Ray Hicks of Beech Moutain, North Carolina Telling
Four Traditional "Jack Tales."* Folk-Legacy, 1963.
(FTA-14) 2s. 12in. 33rpm.

In the true oral tradition Hicks tells "Jack and
the Three Steers"; "Big Man Jack, Killed Seven at
a Whack"; "Jack and the Old Fire Dragon"; and
"Whickety-Whack, into My Sack."

*Richard Chase Tells Three "Jack" Tales from the
Southern Appalachians.* Folk Legacy, 1963. (FTA-6)
2s. 12in. 33rpm.

Chase tells "Jack and the Robbers," "Jack and the
King's Girl," and "Jack and the Three Sillies" to
a group of children from northeastern Tennessee.
The stories are taken from his collection, *Jack
Tales*.

Rootabaga Stories, vol. 1 and vol. 3 (TC 1089, TC
1306) and *How to Tell Corn Fairies When You See 'Em,
and Other Rootabaga Stories,* vol. 2 (TC 1159).
Caedmon, 1958, 1961. 6s. 12in. 33rpm.

Carl Sandburg brings his wonderful stories to life
with his slow-moving rhythmic voice.

Ruth Sawyer, Storyteller. Weston Woods, 1964. (WW
701/702) 4s. 12in. 33rpm.

Sawyer talks about the background to her tales,
gives advice to beginning storytellers, and tells

three folktales--"The Voyage of the Wee Red Cap,"
"The Flea," "The Peddlar of Ballaghadereen"--and
"A Chinese Fairy Tale," by Laurence Housman.

The Star Maiden and Other Indian Tales. CMS Records, 1966. (CMS 500) 2s. 12in. 33rpm.

Anne Pellowski tells four American Indian tales:
"The Star Maiden," "The Punishment of the Raccoon,"
"Snowbird and the Water Tiger," and "Why the Rattle-
snake Sheds Its Skin."

"Storytelling." In *Prelude: Mini-Seminars on Using
Books Creatively, Series 1.* New York: Children's
Book Council, 1975. Cassette.

Augusta Baker talks about the art and technique of
storytelling.

"Storytelling Circle" Recordings. Weston Woods.
Available on 12in. 33rpm or cassette.

The Folktellers, Jay O-Callahan, Jackie Torrance,
Michael Parent, Laura Simms, Donald Davis, David
Holt, Heather Forest, and Diane Wolkstein, are among
the contemporary storytellers who recorded for this
collection. Individual titles in the collection
are available from the producer.

A Storytelling Sampler. National Association for
the Preservation and Perpetuation of Storytelling,
1978. 2s. 12in. 33rpm.

Eleven stories chosen from the National Storytelling
Festival held in Jonesborough, Tennessee. The storytellers are nationally known performers and represent various styles of telling.

Uncle Bouqui: Folktales from Haiti. Folkways/Scho-
lastic Records, 1956. (FP 107) 2s. 10in. 33rpm.

Augusta Baker tells three folktales: "Uncle Bouqui
and Godfather Malice," "Uncle Bouqui Rents a Horse,"
and "Uncle Bouqui Gets Whee-Ai," from Harold
Courlander's book, *Uncle Bouqui of Haiti*.

"Using Folklore as an Introduction to Other Cul-
tures." In *Prelude: Mini-Seminars on Using Books
Creatively, Series 2*. New York: Children's Book
Council, 1976. Cassette.

Anne Pellowski, Director-Librarian at the Information Center on Children's Cultures, U.S. Committee
for UNICEF, talks about using folktale variants
with children.

INDEXES

Author Index